THE DEAD LIVING CHURCH

The Original Concept of the Ekklesia and its perversion

ISAAC K. ARIKAWE

The Dead Living Church
Copyright © 2015 by Isaak K. Arikawe All rights reserved.

No part of this publication may be reproduced, stored in a retrieval system or transmitted in any way by any means, electronic, mechanical, photocopy, recording or otherwise, without the prior permission of the author except as provided by USA copyright law.

All characters appearing in this work are fictitious. Any resemblance to real persons, living or dead, is purely coincidental.

The opinions expressed by the author are not necessarily those of Revival Waves of Glory Books & Publishing.

Published by Revival Waves of Glory Books & Publishing
PO Box 596| Litchfield, Illinois 62056 USA
www.revivalwavesofgloryministries.com

Revival Waves of Glory Books & Publishing is committed to excellence in the publishing industry.

Book design copyright © 2015 by Revival Waves of Glory Books & Publishing. All rights reserved.

Paperback: 978-1-60796-600-5
Hardcover: 978-1-329-15147-5

Published in the United States of America

Table of Contents

Dedication 6
Endorsements 7
Appreciation 13
Author's Note 15
Introduction 18
Chapter One The Origin and Meaning of The Church 22
   THE CHURCH 24
Chapter 2 Jesus' Intention 27
For The Church 27
   JESUS BORROWED THE TERM "CHURCH" 29
   "I WILL BUILD MY CHURCH" 30
Chapter 3 36
The Features Of The Ekklesia 36
   THE PRINCIPLES BEHIND THE BUILDING OF CHRIST'S CHURCH 38
   COMPARISON BETWEEN JESUS' CHURCH AND OTHERS 45
Chapter 4 Jesus' Pattern For Church Building 47
   I WILL BUILD MY CHURCH II 48
   THE GREAT SHIFT 49
   BUILDING ON THE ROCK (The Platform) 51
   BUILDING WITH ROCK (THE STRUCTURE) 53
Chapter 5 The Bricks Versus The Stones 56
   WHICH SYSTEM CONTROLS YOUR OPERATIONS? 58
   BABYLON VERSUS ZION'S OPERATION 61
   THE PRINCIPLES OF BABYLON (BRICKS) 61

Chapter 6 The Church And The Gates of Hell 68

- WHAT ARE THE GATES OF HELL? 69
- WHAT IS HELL? 69
- WHAT ARE GATES? 69
- THE THIRD DIMENSION OF GATES 70
- THE COMBINED OPERATION OF THE THREE DIMENSIONS OF GATES 72
- THE POSITION OF THE CHURCH OVER THE GATES OF HELL 74

Chapter 7 The Church: God's Ambassadors 78

- YOU ARE AN AMBASSADOR 80
- THE NATURE OF OUR ASSIGNMENT 81
- ACCOUNTABILITY OF THE AMBASSADORS 83
- THE CHURCH AND HER WORLD 85
- THE SALT OF THE EARTH 85
- THE SEASONING OF THE EARTH 87
- CAPACITY TO INTERFACE WITH THE REALMS 88
- THE LIGHT OF THE EARTH 89
- THE ILLUMINATION 90
- THE DIRECTION 90

Chapter 8 The Dead-Living Church 93

- CHARACTERISTICS OF THE LIVING CHURCH 94
- NUTRITION 95
- RESPIRATION 96
- EXCRETION 96
- MOVEMENT 98
- SENSITIVITY 98
- GROWTH 99

    REPRODUCTION 101

Chapter 9 **Jesus Outside The Church** 103

    THE SPIRIT WITHIN THE CHURCH 104

    THE BEGINNING OF THE JOURNEY 105

    TYPE 1: THE CHURCH OF EPHESUS 105

    WHAT TO NOTE ABOUT THE CHURCH OF EPHESUS 106

    TYPE 2: THE CHURCH OF SMYRNA 107

    TYPES 3: THE CHURCH OF PERGAMUM 108

    TYPES 4: THE CHURCH OF THYATIRA 109

    TYPE 5: THE CHURCH OF SARDIS 112

    THE CHURCH OF PHILADELPHIA 113

    THE OBEDIENCE OF PHILADELPHIA TYPE OF CHURCH 117

    THE LESSON FOR PHILADELPHIA TYPE OF CHURCH 117

    THE TYPES 7: THE LAODICEA CHURCH 119

    WHAT KEPT JESUS OUTSIDE THE CHURCH 121

    WHAT TO EXPECT WHEN JESUS COMES IN 124

Chapter 10 **Hope For The Remnant** 127

    GOD IS REBUILDING HIS CHURCH 129

    THE ROLE OF INDIVIDUALS 130

    YOU ARE THE CHURCH 132

    THE HEAVEN AND EARTH ARE WAITING 132

About the Book 137

About the Author 138

Other books by the Author 139

Kingdom School of Ministry 144

Dedication

It will be nothing but fraud to dedicate this work to any man. Therefore, it is dedicated to the One who alone is the source of life and revelation- the Holy Spirit- for revealing the mind of God for this hour.

To the people of God all over the world, who is addicted to the truth, not just by preaching it, but by living according to its principles and preparing the way for the coming of the Lord. I pray you will not build in vain.

Endorsements

The parameters for a great Church can never be defined or measured by the Babylonian principles or principles from brilliant minds. The Church was birthed by the Holy Spirit and it can only be sustained by the Holy Spirit. This book and the volume 2; The True Church unveils deeper truth about the true church and the strategies of the devil within the church. If you desire truth go for it.

Dr. D. K. Olukoya,
General Overseer,
Mountain of Fire & Miracles Ministries

"Until you are able to understand the Chemistry of your Body, you'll be depressed by the Biology of this world"

All Christians must settle down to know how the body of Christ (Church) operates, otherwise we'll be filled with the theology of the letters. That is the sense in this Book: A must read for every Believer. The Dead Living Church is end time prescription for the body of Christ. See you on top!!!

Olu Fred Kehinde
Presiding Bishop,
Power House Chapel International,
Cologne, Germany

I salute the courage of Isaac Arikawe in confronting the mediocrity of the present church and its lack of clarity and perception in living up to its prophetic mandate. The Dead-Living Church offers a profound definition of the concept and purpose of the church, and its relevance to human existence, with an insightful historical background. Thank you for a job well done, Pastor Isaac, and more grease to your elbow!

Tayo Ladejo,
Senior Pastor,
The Governing Church,
Ikoyi Lagos.

Isaac Arikawe, a prolific author and teacher of God's word, in The Dead-Living Church, exposes the error of men who have turned Christ's Church into their own personal estates and enterprises, using the instrumentalities of satanically motivated manipulation, worldly practices, marketing strategies and the greed for money, titles and position to tear apart the heart of the Chief Cornerstone of the Church, Jesus Christ. Moreover, this book highlights the apostolic dimensions on how individual and corporate churches can become cutting edge pillars and grounds of truth to bring forth the anticipated glorious church. This book is a must read for all church leaders, workers and everyone craving for reformation and revelation.

David T. Adeoye,
Founding President,
Heaven Rules Prophetic Ministries.

This book gives a very detailed explanation of what Jesus intended His Church to be. This book has a lot of striking captions. The author has successfully given us a picture of what the Church of Jesus will be like in the days to come. He also points out that in spite of the Church's imperfect state, there still remains a remnant preserved by God for Himself.

Tokunbo Johnson,
Founding Pastor,
The Capstone Church, Lagos.

The church is no doubt the body of Christ and also His bride. He walks in the midst watching and seeing all that is done in His body. This book has gone ahead to describe the Church as a living body, explaining the way the body functions in order to remain healthy and functional so as to fulfill her mission on earth. As you read this book you will find the situation that best fits your position in the body

Rev Azuka Ogbolumani
Chaplain,
Chapel of Christ our Light,
University of Lagos.

The Bible says that if the foundations be destroyed, what shall the righteous do? (Psalm 11:3) The word "Church" today has come to mean a lot of things to a lot of people. That the church is dead or alive today is a consequence of the fundamental, foundational belief of the propagators and followers of "The Church". Isaac Arikawe's "The Dead Living Church" and "The True Church" take us to the origins of the concept and purpose of the church and its relevance to our existence to help us gain understanding of God's will for His Church. You will find this series most revealing.

Emeka Nwako
Pastor-in-charge, RCCG,
Adonai Parish, Area 70,
Lagos Province 12

In ministry, there are those who are called of God and there are also those who call themselves. The fact, however, is that the difference between them is usually clear. Pastor Isaac Arikawe is called with a clear apostolic mandate to set in order the things that are wanting in the body of Christ. This truth is exemplified in the message of this book. This masterpiece in your hand is loaded with the priceless truth of all ages and also with the power of endless life. As you read a line, you will want to read more. If you are sure you are going somewhere as a believer and you are tired of religion, this book is for you!

Sola Iwaeni,
Senior Pastor,
Positive Impact Christian Centre,
Lagos.

I believe this book is real, spiritual and relevant to all at this time and season. To the Church, it calls us to understand our God-given assignment and seek to accomplish it speedily. To the world, it invites the unsaved into the reality of the kingdom of God and of His dear Son, Jesus Christ. To everyone it reveals that the kingdom is the sole reason we have been created by our Maker. I recommend this book to whoever cares to do the WILL of God.,

Aremu Ayobami
Essex, United Kingdom.

The paradoxical exactitude which is comprehensively explained by Isaac Arikawe in his books, The Dead-Living Church and The True Church cannot be over-emphasized. It explains core essence of most church people today. The messages of the books are basically a clarion call for those who have been enmeshed in religious activities without any spiritual productivity to turn a new leaf. Having gone through the books, I can gladly recommend them to anyone who is a true seeker of truth. The explanation of the etymology of the word "Church" gives the reader a platform of better understanding of the concept. Also, the category of our local assemblies today, as seen in the Book of Revelation sets a platform for self-examination for those who think godliness is gain. In all, these books, without doubt would set you at the cutting edge of reformation, revolution and revival. These are must-read books for pastors and parishioners, ministers and members of local assemblies and for those who have been called into the ministry.

Wale Odeniyi,
Author, The Kingdom Life Book

Brother Arikawe is an accomplished writer whom I have known years back. I am glad God is using him to shape the crooked roads which the Church of Christ has trod upon for decades. My old crony, Isaac Arikawe, has hazarded his life on water and land, together with me and Rev. H.A. Benjamin to see the undiluted gospel of Christ preached to lost souls. I cannot help giving the brief ghostly smiles when I remember a non-swimmer, Isaac Arikawe, shivering and almost falling into the ocean, yet preaching Jesus to riverine dwellers in Ondo State of Nigeria. Arikawe is a positive generational time bomb in the hands of the Most High. I'm not surprised at what God is revealing through him about the church of this generation. I am waiting for more spiritual explosions!

Evangelist Kunle Omosehin,
Newham, E6, 5JJ, London, UK.

Appreciation

I especially thank the Almighty God for inspiring me to write this great book. Thank you Father for making me an oracle at this time.

My appreciation also goes to my parents, Chief. and Mrs. Adesola Arikawe and my beloved siblings for all their care, support and investments. Also to my in-laws, the Ogunniran's, you are the best.

I appreciate Rev. and Mrs. H. A. Benjamin for helping me to discover my potential and putting me through life. To my covenant friend, Pastor and Mrs. David Adeoye, thank you for believing so much in me. God bless you. To Pastor and Mrs. Sola Iwaeni, another covenant friend and brother, thank you for your commitment, true love and encouragement to my life, ministry and to this publication.

Much appreciation goes to my pastors, Pastor & Pastor (Mrs.) Tokunbo and Funmi Johnson, for being there for me all the time. Pastor and Mrs. Ade Ewunuga, I appreciate your fatherly and mentorship style; it is not common. My appreciation also goes to Pastor Abiodun Oso and Rev. Azuka Ogbolumani, the Chaplain, Chapel of Christ Our Light, University of Lagos, Nigeria. Your impact in my life will remain forever. Much thanks also to Dr. Akeremale, Tosin Aremu, Chidi Okwonkwo, Richard Ugbede, Tunde Aremu, Mr Tinuoye Johnson. I value our relationship.

My special thanks to my friend, Wale Odeniyi, for your sleepless night of proof- reading this book. My God will reward you. God bless Orishebemio Awala, Sam O. Salau, for your encouragement and supports towards this publication. God bless

Mr. Seun Onanuga for taking out time to edit this work. To all my other friends whose names are not in this publication, I appreciate and love you all. God will always be with you all. I also appreciate Pastor Ndukuba of the MFM Church who took the time to do the final editing of these books. God bless you, sir.

I want to say thank you and may God really bless you. A special thanks to Dr. D.K Olukoya for your special interest, advice and support in bringing this publication to reality. You are God-sent and your kind of heart for the kingdom is rare. May God continue to uphold you.

To my wife, my treasure, the best thing that has ever happened to me after my salvation, you are indeed God-sent. Thank you for being so patient in making all the necessary corrections. Life without you would have been meaningless. Love you so much.

Author's Note

I have come to understand that regardless of how perverse a generation has become, it is not beyond redemption. All that God requires for the restoration of a people that are lost is hearts that are willing. The chapters ahead establish that although God can use anyone to fulfill His purpose, He would not use every one. He has criteria and parameters that are best known to Him. He once used a donkey to speak to Balaam, a raven to feed Elijah and a big fish to take Jonah to Nineveh. He could even use stones if men refuse to worship Him, but He is looking for men! Therefore, it is a great privilege that God has transferred the burden in His heart to our own hearts and has caused our eyes to see what is going on in the realm of the spirit. The message of this book is not what I can boast about; it is a function of the grace of God. It is not by human efforts, calculations or intelligence. It is not a professional work, but a prophetic one. God only chose to reveal His mind. For this reason I give all glory and praise to Him for the inspiration in this book. The Father has revealed His will to us through the help of the Holy Spirit.

On September 29, 2001, I was invited by Pastor David T. Adeoye to minister at the Nigeria Youth Christian Movement Conference, Lagos. The meeting was attended by youths from different churches, campuses and groups. The conference was tagged "The WIND 2001." From my interactions with the organizers of the program, I could see that they were apostolic and prophetic inclined. They wanted my messages to be centered on the "Move of God." I did pray towards the program, believing God for what He would have in mind for His people. While I was preparing in prayer for this conference, the Holy Spirit spoke to me expressly about what to speak on: THE CHURCH ON THE ROCK. He opened my heart to understand what this was all about, explaining that the church could only survive by continuous revelation from God. Jesus said in John 5:19, "I tell you the truth; the Son can do nothing by himself. He does only what he sees the Father doing." He said again in Matthew 16:18, "Now I say to you that you are Peter (which means 'rock'), and upon this rock I will build my church, and all the powers of Hell will not conquer it."

As I was introduced and given the microphone to speak, I saw a crowd of young men and women who were only religiously inclined. God then said to me, "See how people are religiously seeking me, whereas all I need is just a relationship." After this, the only thing I could remember was the statement, which the Holy Spirit put in my heart. I kept on declaring it without considering my feelings or the feelings of my audience: "The church remains my problem, not the devil, because the devil has been defeated but the church is dying." I kept on repeating this until the end of my message. I eventually handed over the microphone and left the arena with a great burden. God told me, "I want you to put all that I showed you and the one I will still reveal to you in a book."

Beloved, from 2001 till 2008, this book has been a great burden in my heart amongst other assignments God has given to me. I have always been teaching this message ever since in most of the conferences where I was booked to speak freely by God's grace. On a daily basis, revelations on the subject of the church of Jesus continued to increase in my heart by the Holy Ghost. Sometimes I abandon other things that occupy my time so that this gracious work of God can be published.

This book, The Dead-Living Church, is just a prelude to what God actually wants to open unto us. The main message is contained in the volume 2- "The True Church." The things that

God revealed to me are so much that it would be too voluminous for one book. I had to split the message into two parts. Please, open your heart to God and I believe that the Holy Spirit will bear witness with your spirit. I also believe that this book will cause an adjustment in our lives so that God can have His way in us and through us. One thing I am very sure of is that you would read this book and recommend it to others, including the volume II (The True Church). Just to remind you again, God has your interest at heart. He loves you!

Isaac Arikawe K.

Introduction

"Jesus replied, "You are blessed, Simon, son of John, because my Father in heaven has revealed this to you. You did not learn this from any human being. Now, I say you that you are Peter (which means rock) and upon this rock I will build my Church and all the power of hell will not conquer it."
Matthew 16:17-18

"...I know all the things you do, but that you have a reputation for being alive- but you are dead. Wake up! Strengthen what little remains, for even what is left is almost dead. I find that your actions do not meet the requirement."
Revelations 3:1-2

The dead-living church is an inspiration from the Holy Spirit. The caption expresses the heaviness in the heart of Jesus concerning the church today. You may question the reason for such a caption and wonder if the phrase does make any sense at all. Whatever may be your opinion as touching the issue, the truth is that the Holy Spirit is trying to pass a message across to the church through this book. You will come to understand these things as you read on. More clarifications will also be made in the Volume II of the book.

The Dead-Living Church is a spiritual paradox. It is a phrase which, although it sounds absurd, has a lot of truth in it. The phrase is absurd in the sense that it seems neither logical nor sensible. It sounds completely ridiculous. It is also an oxymoron, that is, it involves placing two contrasting words together to pass a message across to the audience. This implies that God has a picture in mind and He is using this phrase to paint the picture for those with prophetic eyes and hearts so that they can understand. It may be hard to imagine that something could be both dead and living at the same time.

Jesus declared a great visionary statement over two thousand years ago: Now I say to you that you are Peter (which means 'rock' and upon this I will build my church and all the power of hell (gates of Hades) will not conquer it." (Matthew 16.18). From Jesus' statement, you will observe that some types of churches must have been in existence before He came on the scene to say He would build His own church. Secondly, you will also discover that none of the disciples asked him what He meant by the word "Church," meaning that they were already familiar with the term. This means that the word was not in any way new to them. Thirdly, the word "Church" is not a religious term. It is actually a secular and political term. The Greek word "Ekklesia" means "The assembly," "the called out", "the congregation" or "the parliament," in contemporary terms. The Greek established parliaments long before the birth of Jesus. There was an assembly of the citizens of the Greek Nation (see Acts 19:32, 39). It was in this Greek parliament that issues beyond individuals or selected groups were resolved. The verdicts given by these assemblies were usually the final after the government had endorsed their recommendations. Fourthly, the Greek translation was used over one hundred times in the scriptures, especially in the Old Testament. (1 Samuel 19:20 and Numbers 22:4). In the New Testament, the early church saw themselves as "The called out ones" (Hebrew 1:1-2) and as the legitimate children of Israel- those who are born of God through the new covenant in Jesus.

Jesus was therefore introducing another concept entirely different from what people in the world were used to. Although other churches and assemblies were established constitutionally,

He said, "I will build my own kind of church." Many people misinterpret this statement by translating or relating the word "build" to physical, civil engineering structures. No! Jesus was not talking about physical building; He was rather talking about a different kind of people- a holy nation, those whose hearts can never be corrupted, damaged, subjected and limited by the systems of this world.

No doubt, when purpose is not known, abuse is inevitable. When the definition of a concept is not clearly understood, it will never be used for its original intent. It is also clear that death and decaying may not always happen simultaneously. If there are any malfunctioning parts in a system, that system will die gradually. And once the system is dead, the decaying process will also be gradual. Just as diseases could bring about malfunctioning in the life of an individual, lack of understanding could also hinder the church from fulfilling the mandate of God on earth, thereby bringing about the operation of the spirit of death.

In this book, so much is revealed about the dead and the living church. As you read along, you will also see the characteristics of both kinds of churches. Although human parameters and standards for measuring what a living church is may differ from one individual to another, we must still go on to find what the truth is. The church of Jesus has been operating on human senses for hundreds of years now. The Holy Spirit, who is the guide of the church, has been somewhat sidelined while opinion and experience of experts have taken the place of the Prophetic in the church of Jesus. The oneness in the assembly of Jesus Christ has been divided by self-centredness, lust for position and titles, money and fame, racism and tribalism, educational status and "connection", to mention a few. Politics has become the order of the day. The purpose of the church is to reconcile the world back to the Creator through our lifestyles and kingdom values, but it is sad that the church is also beginning to pursue shadows instead of reality.

In this book, deep truths about the church of Jesus are revealed and the consequences of deadness in the church are also mentioned. It is painful to see that the perfect church is yet to emerge on the earth, although the whole heaven and the earth have been waiting for her manifestation. The church is responsible for enforcing the will of God on the earth. The church is likewise responsible for the delay in the coming of Jesus. It's not the devil. The Bible says "For he must remain in heaven until the time for the final restoration (restitution) of all things, as God promised long ago through his holy prophets" (Act 3:21). This means that, Jesus will not return, until the church has dealt with the global issues, thereby subjecting men to the authority of Heaven. It is rather unfortunate that many believers are praying and waiting for an opportunity to escape from the world, not knowing that they have been chosen by God to take authority on earth and teach all nations the ways of God until the kingdoms of this world become the kingdom of our God and His Christ.

This book is an eye opener. It will cause every reader to experience a reformation in the mind. It could also serve as a manual for self-examination and as a guide as you proceed to build for God on earth. The pattern you are building with, the kind of materials amongst other things, will determine whether your work will stand the test of time or whether your labor will be in vain. I urge you to open up your heart so that the Holy Spirit can do something new through you. I also pray that the God of heaven will cause you to encounter the truth. As you go through this piece, I pray that the eyes of your understanding will be enlightened beyond its scope so that you will long to do only the will of God on the face of the earth.

Isaac Arikawe K.

Chapter One

The Origin and Meaning of The Church

"The true measure of a living church is not in setting denominational goals, but in creating generational relevance."

"The human body has many parts, but the many parts make up one whole body. So it is with the body of Christ."
1Corinthians 12:15

The question, "What is church?" Is one that every believer must have an accurate answer to. Sometimes the exact meaning of a word can be easily understood if it is traced to its root meaning in another language. The word "church" is not originally an English word; it was translated into the English language from Greek. The Greek word for it is "Ekklesia," and the word also has two meanings: "called out" and "Assembly." The Roman government, for example, had their own Ekklesia, which always had the final say over every issue that could not be resolved by other parties. These assemblies were not religious establishments but they had the authority to approve and disapprove claims, proposals, ideas, policies, budgets and other issues relating to the welfare of the people of their kingdom.

"If Demetrius and the craftsman have a case against them, (Gaius and Aristarchus, who were Paul's traveling companions) the courts are in session and the officials can hear the cases at once. Let them make formal charges. And if there are complaints about other matters, they can settle in a Legal assembly. I am afraid; we are in danger of being charged with rioting by the Roman government, since there is no cause for all this commotion. And if Rome demands an explanation, we won't know what to say". Then he dismissed them, and they dispersed." Acts 19:38-41

In the above portion of the Bible, the word translated as legal assembly, which other versions refer to as lawful assembly of the Roman government is not a religious term. If we want to interpret literally, it is a secular, administrative and political term. Therefore, as we move on in this expository journey, we would do well to keep this in mind. We should keep the original meanings, the Ekklesia (called out ones) or the assembly in our hearts whenever we come across the word "church" as we read on.

The original Greek word for church was used more than one hundred times in the Greek translation of the Old Testament till the time of Jesus. Its Hebrew translation is "qahal" and it simply means "assembly." The word was used in various places throughout the scriptures. Deuteronomy 9:10, reads:

"And the LORD delivered unto me two tables of stone written with finger of God; and on them was written according to all the words, which the LORD spoke with you in the mount out of the midst of the fire, in the day of the assembly." (KJV)

The use of this term in the Old Testament, referring to the people of God is very essential to our understanding of the term "church "in the New Testament.

THE CHURCH

Going by the points we have already established about the church, we can see clearly that the term "church" is not actually what we often define it to be today; and if we find it difficult to get the definition right, there is possibility that the purpose of the church will be misunderstood. Many scholars and religious authorities could not trace the origin of this term, which was one of the fundamental reasons for the deficiency in the power and efficacy of the church today. Let's quickly look at the English usage of the word 'church' along with the Greek's.

In contemporary English, the word church dominates the ecclesiological vocabulary. It comes through German and Latin and from the Greek word Kyriakon, meaning, "That which belongs to the Lord." In the New Testament (Greek) Ekklesia (always translated in English as 'church') is by no means so dominating or central a term. Ekklesia (Latin spelling) was used primarily to designate a particular communal reality, not to describe its qualitative aspects. Where the distinctive qualities and dimensions of community life were intended, other terms proved more flexible and evocative. In comparison with these other terms, Ekklesia was relatively neutral and colorless, conveying only little theological meaning. It was open to use, without a basic shift in meaning, both by unbelievers and believers. Even among those writers who made use of the word Ekklesia, other terms were more expressive of the reality at hand.

Moreover, some people (scholars and theologians) did not do thorough justice to the word "church" because they narrowed their definition of the contemporary use without searching deeply into the origin of the word in Greek, Hebrew or Latin. If they did, they would have also understood, based on what we established earlier, that the Roman Government did not refer to the church as a religious body, but as an assembly, a set of people selected for a particular task, or the called out ones. You can call them the house of the senate that represents constituencies or kingdoms, which gives final verdicts on every matter and policy. This actually depends on the case or issues concerned.

As I said earlier, some got it wrong in the perspective at which they defined the church and the same act determines the way they relate to the subject matter. For instance, Oxford Advanced Learner's Dictionary defines church as follows:

(1)   A building where Christians go to worship; a church tower.

(2)   A service or services in the church, that is, how often you go to the church

(3)   A particular group of Christians: the Anglican Church; the Catholic Church, The Methodist Church; as a denomination.

Beloved, do you accept or agree with these definitions? Regardless of what you think, as we continue on the journey, the Holy Spirit will give you more understanding.

Painfully, the wrong understanding of the word "church" has given rise to the formation of other words and terminologies, which are not supposed to be part of the framework of the Church. If truly church is Ekklesia, "called out" and "assembly", then how did we come about the words/phrases below:

(1)   Churchgoers: persons who go to church services regularly (Dictionary meaning).

(2)   Churchman (clergyman)

(3)   Church warden- (Orthodox/Protestant) person who is chosen by members of a church to take care of church property and money.

Frankly speaking, if the word Ekklesia is the root meaning of the word church, then it means the church is a people (living beings), not a building as most dictionaries define it. It is neither a denomination, nor a group of believers, but a people that carries out some well-defined functions. It refers to individuals, groups of people, set aside or called out for a particular task. It will not make any sense if certain people are "called out" but are not carrying out any specific assignment. Every calling or separation must be with a specific and a defined purpose. The church is therefore not just a denomination, but also a people with a definite purpose stated by the authority that called them out or set them aside.

Chapter 2

Jesus' Intention For The Church

"A true church is one whose revolutionary impact is first felt within her immediate community."

There was a believer in Joppa named Tabitha (which in Greek in Dorcas) she was always doing kind things for others and helping the poor"
Acts 9:46

Without doubt, Jesus of Nazareth still remains the most popular and influential personality that ever lived on the surface of the earth. Many people in the world have either at one time or the other heard about Him. This does not necessarily mean all those who have heard about Him believed in the work of His sacrifice for humanity, but somehow they must have heard about His name.

History records that Jesus, though He was God in nature, lived among men; he dined and wined with men. He related with all kinds of people: families, disciples, Jews, the poor and the rich, religious leaders, politicians, etc. He also worked with Joseph (his earthly father) as a carpenter. This means that He was dealing with His father's clients as well. History shows that He studied and practiced even the Jewish culture and religious laws; He studied the administration of nations, lifestyles of people, languages of every sector, etc., to the extent that it became so paramount in His teachings. He used the words, languages and events that people could easily relate with and understand to teach the messages of God's kingdom.

On many occasions, Jesus taught and corrected the people's impression by quoting the books of the law and the prophets (the Old Testament). If He had not studied these things, He would not have been quoting them as references while teaching. For example, in order to describe the relevance of the people of the Kingdom, he likened them to salt and light, things that people relate with everyday (Matthew 5:13-16). He taught on the subject of divorce by first quoting from the Law of Moses, found in Deuteronomy 24:1. He quoted it accurately for them before He then set forth the teachings of the new dispensation (Matthew 5:31-32). He dealt with issues of temperament. He redefined who a murderer is contrary to what the Law of Moses explained it to be based on its standard of judgment and righteousness. In the

New Testament, he said that merely calling someone a fool or an idiot is equivalent to murder. He established this by quoting from Exodus 20:3; Deuteronomy 5:17 and Matt. 5:21-22. All these are to establish to us that He made a correction by first studying what people believed in and lived by.

Let us take another case as the last on Jesus' interaction with this world- its operating system, people and their various cultures. In Matthew 8:5-13, Jesus met a Roman officer- a controller of soldiers- who had a very sick servant and requested Jesus' assistance in healing him. In the course of their discussion, Jesus discovered a great virtue in this Roman officer. He declared that he had never seen his kind of faith, not even among the people of Israel who claimed that the patriarchs Abraham, Isaac and Jacob were their fathers. What we can see in the established principles in the above scriptures is that Jesus dealt with people from all backgrounds and cultures. Although He was a Jew, He understood the Romans more than the citizens of Rome. Little wonder He could borrow terminologies from other languages and cultures.

JESUS BORROWED THE TERM "CHURCH"

Jesus was on earth for a defined mission, which was to preach the gospel of the Kingdom and destroy the works of hell. Throughout the scriptures, His message centered round "the Gospel of the kingdom of God" (Matthew 4:23; 9:35; Mark 1:14-15). He declared His mission statement saying, "I must preach the kingdom of God in other towns too, because for this purpose I have been sent" (Luke 4:43 NKJV). In order to make His vision and mission, clear to the people, He decided to borrow words and terminologies from natural phenomena and from the people's cultures. He likened the church to things like salt, light, etc.

Moreover, it should no longer be a subject of argument to ask if people were familiar with the word "church" (Ekklesia/

assembly) before the days of Jesus; otherwise, there would have been a need for the listeners ask questions about the meaning of each word that sounded strange to them in order to have a clear understanding. If this were the case, He Himself would have told them beforehand what the word(s) might mean. This is to prevent the listeners from getting confused and the essence of His message being misunderstood.

"I WILL BUILD MY CHURCH"

"Now I say to you that you are Peter (which means 'rock), and upon this rock (of revelation) I will build my church and all the powers of hell (gates of Hades) will not conquer it. And I will give you the keys of the kingdom of Heaven. Whatever you forbid (bind or lock) on earth will be forbidden in heaven, and whatever you permit (loose or open) on earth will be permitted in heaven. Matthew 16:18-19

If, for instance, I decide that I am going to design my own car, what will that suggest to you? Does it suggest to you that I am going to manufacture a particular brand of car similar to what I have seen somewhere else? Or does it suggest to you that I want to design something that eyes have never seen on earth before, so that I can call it my own branded car? If you are still thinking of what to answer, then pause for a minute and interpret the statement based on your own understanding.

The truth is this, when I say, "I am going to design my own car," these are some of the things that it could suggest to you:

- I must have seen a sample of something called a car before.
- I must have understood the purpose and the functions of a car.
- I must have had a clear understanding of the ability and capacity of the already existing type of car.

- I must have been aware of the efficiency and limits of the already existing car.
- I must have discovered the shortcoming, deficiency or challenges of the already designed car.

With all these said above, there must be functions or something I must have discovered which I need or which I am looking for in a car that the already existing car(s) does not possess. Therefore, if I have a genuine purpose in designing another brand of car, the questions below must be taken into consideration:

- What do I really need in a car?
- What capacity and ability am I looking for?
- Also, if the one I am planning to design will not be better in any sense of judgment compared to the already existing one, it does not make any sense re-designing another brand.

Let us not forget that it was the statement of Jesus, "I will build my church" that led us to the case study above for our proper understanding as we proceed on this journey.

At this juncture, I do not know the part you belong to, whether we share the same or different opinions. The truth is that there were churches (assemblies) that Jesus saw before concluding that He would build His own kind of church (assembly/Ekklesia), the kind that had never been seen in the world before then. This is a church with a different "technology," to be "configured" or built with the best "software" that can never be corrupted by the system of this world. It is a church with an inbuilt anti-virus that is competent of handling or subduing any "virus" from the pit of hell.

It is imperative that you bear in mind that there were also other churches apart from that of the Roman government, such as the church (assembly) of the Israelites (God's people) in the wilderness.

"The Lord gave me the two tablets on which God had written with his own finger all the words he had spoken to you from the heart of the fire when you were assembled at the Mountain" Deuteronomy 9:10

Other versions like King James Version concluded the last part of this scripture with "… out of the midst of the fire, in the day of the assembly."

We can see the nature and deficiency of this kind of church when we read down to Deuteronomy. 9:12: "Then the Lord said to me, 'Get up! Go down immediately, for the people (Ekklesia) you brought out of Egypt have corrupted themselves. How quickly they have turned away from the way I commanded them to live! They have melted gold and made an idol for themselves?"

The classes of the assemblies we have seen so far cannot fit into the technology that Jesus was planning to invent, that is, His own kind of church, which will rule over the earth, establishing the kingdom of the Father. This was the primary point of all his teachings and messages, the assembly that would judge the devil on earth by their operating system (lifestyle and dominion). The kind of church Jesus was talking about building was the kind that Prophet Obadiah saw and declared thousands of years before Jesus came:

"And saviours shall come up on mount Zion to judge the mount of Esau; and the kingdom shall be the Lord's" Obadiah Vs 21 KJV

There are four major words to be considered in the passage above: The saviours, Zion, Esau and Kingdom. We shall look at these words, one after the other.

Saviours: This is plural and it tells us that it was not referring to Jesus. This also means that the era of one-man-show has gone. The emphasis of heaven today is corporate anointing- the assembly. It is not the kind of assembly where God will be speaking to Pastor Moses alone in the wilderness while the congregation will be completely alienated from hearing Him. God is raising the assembly of Joshua, where everybody will be involved in taking the battle to the gates of the enemy. (See Joshua 3:5-6, 13).

Jesus would not have made a mistake by saying He was going to build His own kind of Church that would show the world the express image and the power of God and show the kingdom of darkness the manifold wisdom of God. It is by this that He will bring the whole earth to the lordship and worship of our God - as the main function of king and priest, which was the level Jesus was targeting for the kind of assembly (church) he was planning to build. This will not be for the priests (pastors), a particular set of people alone but every member of the assembly. This was the revelation that Peter caught:

"But you are not like that, for you are a chosen people. You are a royal priests (every member of the assembly) a holy nation; God's very own possession (My church). As a result, you can show others the goodness of God, for he called you out of the darkness into his wonderful light. Don't forget that Ekklesia (the church) means the assembly and also the "called out." 1 Peter 2:9

Zion: the second key word, Zion, in the spirit, typifies the assembly of the saints, the people of God; the redeemed, which can also be called the church. What Jesus had in mind in redesigning the concept and the technology of the church was to raise men (saviours) from this assembly that will present the true values of God on earth and stand as a singular standard that will pull down the works of the enemy.

Esau: The third keyword is Esau. The Mount of Esau stands for the mount of wickedness, corruption and perverse generation. When everything would have been put under control, the Kingdom, which is the fourth key will come to stay. It was the same prophetic future (insight), which God opened the eyes of John to see; that it shall come to pass, when Jesus' kind of Church is built on earth, and the kingdoms of this world shall become the Lord's.

"Then the seventh angel blew his trumpet, and there were loud voices shouting in heaven. The world has now become the kingdom of our Lord and of His Christ, and He will reign forever and ever." Revelations 11:15

Beloved, I believe the Holy Spirit would have illuminated your hearts to a point where you should now agree and see that Jesus had a distinctive picture in mind as regards the type of church he wanted to build compared to the existing ones on earth. It may be the Romans', which were political and subject to human influences and specific geographical locations the Roman territories or the church in the wilderness that could not withstand corruption. The "technology" Jesus had in mind to establish in the church in order to demonstrate the full dominion on earth without any geographical barriers has not been seen on earth for now. We shall proceed to look at the full content of Jesus' kind of church and other churches (assemblies) as the Spirit of the Lord grants us deeper revelation.

Kingdom: The word "kingdom" derives its meaning from two important words: 'king' and 'domain'. The word 'king' talks about rulership, dominion, authority, power and governance. In the same vein, the word 'domain' defines territories, boundaries, locations, realms, etc. Kingdom is far bigger than the church. Kingdom refers to the entire realm of God's creation, where rulership and authority are needed; it may be physical or spiritual.

When the Savior shall rise and take their full responsibilities in all facets of life, globally, then the kingdom shall be the Lord's.

Chapter 3

The Features Of The Ekklesia

"Any structure or design that functions outside a defined fundamental process and original intention of the designer is called malfunction."

"Now these are the gifts Christ gave to the church: the apostles, the prophets, the evangelists, the pastors, and the teachers. Their responsibilities is to equip God's people to do His work and build up the church, the body of Christ.
Ephesians 4:11-12

It is expedient for us to first consider the functional features of different Ekklesia before we can really understand what makes Jesus' kind or class of Ekklesia to be peculiar. Also, it would be very important to put some things into consideration when looking at the feature of the Ekklesia.

- Why were they established?
- What power, constitution or law established them?
- How relevant were they to their environment?
- What were the limits of their operations?
- What was the extent of power and authority vested in them?
- What were the things that caught Jesus' attention about them?
- Were there certain things that Jesus picked or emulated from any of these Ekklesia?

It is true that the identity of a man can never be far from his operations. I mean, closely looking at a man's passion, burden, beliefs and operations, one can easily tell who he is. Dear reader, don't also forget that the essence of this search is to get us a conclusion by the Spirit of God where we can both see the difference between the Jesus' type of church and any other kind. Never to forget that many groups are called out as well (there are many assemblies). In the course of extracting this truth, it will also be important to find the true origin and the basis for Jesus' statement, "I will build my church."

When Jesus came to the region of Caesarea Philippi; he asked his disciples, who do people say that the son of man is? Well, they replied, some say John the Baptist, and some say Elijah and other say Jeremiah or one of the other prophets. Then he asked them, but who do you say I am? Simon Peter answered, you are the

Messiah (Christ), the son of the living God. Jesus replied, you are blessed, Simon, son of John (bar-Jonah), because my father in heaven has revealed this to you. You did not learn this from any human being. Now I say to you that you are Peter (which means 'rock'), and upon this rock I will build my church, and all the powers of hell (the gates of Hades) will not conquer it. I will give you the keys of the kingdom of heaven. Whatever you forbid (binds, or locks) on earth will be forbidden in heaven, and whatever you permit (loose, or open) on earth will be permitted in heaven. Matthew 16:13-19

From the above scriptures, you will agree with me the public opinion and the conclusion reached by Jesus Christ that if a man's personality and identity could be misunderstood then his messages and philosophies would definitely be misunderstood as well. Hence, in getting the true identity of Jesus' kind of church, we would do a little comparison between the proposed church He desired to build and the already existing ones (the wilderness and Roman government Ekklesia). But before then, it will do us much good, grant us more understanding, if we can pick out some principles from the scriptures above: Matthew 16:13-19.

THE PRINCIPLES BEHIND THE BUILDING OF CHRIST'S CHURCH

Let us not forget that Jesus appeared as the Son of God in human form to rescue the world from its fallen state. He was on earth with a definite purpose, which was to restore man to his original position of sonship, restoring to him the lost dominion and authority to rule this world- the dominion given to him in the Garden of Eden. (Genesis 1:26-28). He therefore came for people and He also need people to accomplish this task. He chose few disciples to walk with Him and to learn His ways so that He could later send them forth to reach the world. He prepared them so that they would continue from where He stopped. No wonder He said, "The work that I did, you will do also, and even greater works you will do." John 14:12

In verse 13 of Matthew chapter 16, Jesus was sought to know the public opinion about Himself through His disciples. Don't forget that there shouldn't be any disparity between the messenger and his message, otherwise integrity is gone and it is not of God. The way a man operates is what reveals His identity and His values. Jesus knew that the people's opinion about Him would determine how well they would respond to His message. He knew He could not reach out to them so well if they did not know who He really was and what He had come to do. The same question is what I pose to you, beloved: who do people say you are?

In verse 14, the disciples responded that people took Him for Elijah, Jeremiah or one of the great prophets. We can see that there were some operations in His ministry that the public could trace or relate to those of the old prophets. The public must have seen the light of God in Him for them to compare Him to other notable men of God. Although these people's opinions were quite correct- it shows that they thought Him. The truth is that their judgment was not accurate, and this is where Jesus was going to address. This also shows that Jesus did not clearly declare who He was to the people; He wanted God to reveal His personality to them.

In verse 15, He said to His disciples, "Who do you say I am?" The Bible does not record that any of them made guesses. There was total silence until the next verse where Peter spoke. This also means that people could be very close to Jesus and still not know who He really is. He was trying to teach His disciples and the church today that the mysteries of God are to be discovered by revelation, not by information and logical conclusions. This was the principle He was trying to teach the disciples. This also implies that whatever a preacher teaches his congregation cannot be clearly understood except they also build a personal relationship with the Father, from whom the preacher draws his inspiration.

In verse 16, Peter answered after a long time of general silence: "You are the Messiah (the Christ), the Son of the living God."

Before we consider the principles in the response of Jesus, let us compare the responses of the public in verses 13 and 16. The public considered Him to be a prophet- someone who had been sent to them as a mouthpiece of God. Peter, however recognized Him as the Christ (the Anointed), the Messiah, the One all Israel and the world had been waiting for, although they never knew.

In verse 17, Jesus replied, "You are blessed, Simon, son of John (bar-Jonah), because my father in heaven has revealed this to you. You did not learn this from any human being." Please, beloved reader, take this verse very seriously; this point is very heavy and can change the course of your life and ministry. Jesus was overwhelmed by the reply of Peter; He couldn't help but declare a blessing over him. The statement, "You are blessed" could be interpreted, "You have got everything you need in order to change your world." This was what God told Abraham in Genesis 12:12. He said that He would bless him (Abraham) and that through him all the nations of the earth would be blessed.

Every true blessing can only come from God. What Jesus meant by "You are blessed" is beyond physical things; being blessed also means having access to the things of heaven. Jesus knew Peter had never gone to any theological school or had any formal training like the Pharisees and the Scribes, yet Jesus declared woe (a great curse) on the Pharisees and the Scribes (the so-called men of God of that era). These were people who were educated in the things of God, conversant with the law and who also taught the people. This reveals to us that the things of the Father cannot be got by human senses. Another version refers to this as "flesh and blood." It does not come by theological studies, rather, it comes by true connection to the Spirit of the living God. This also connotes that what Peter said was a mystery because Jesus said, "My Father in heaven has revealed this to you." The word' revealed means to unveil or to uncover something sealed up.

Friends, I will suggest that you pray for yourself and for the Church of God, that God will cause us to align with the Holy Spirit so that our labor will not be in vain.

In verse 18, Jesus said, "Now I say to you that you are Peter (which means rock), and upon this rock I will build my church, and all powers of hell will not conquer it".

Don't forget that this same Peter was known as Simon Bar-Jonah, meaning Simon the son of Jonah. The name Simon means unstable, wavering, unpredictable, inconsistent, etc. What it means literally is that Simon is undependable by name, which interprets his life style. Jesus changed his name to Peter (meaning rock): something reliable, predictable, stable; something you can bank on or lean on.

This tells us that God does not relate with us based on our external circumstances, but on our internal identity in Him. Jesus could see something good in Simon and that was why He changed his name to something that heaven could relate with. Do not forget Peter did not change the name by himself, but heaven changed the wrong identity to what would bring blessing to him and his world.

Beloved, what kind of identity do you carry in the spirit? The devil may be able to prevail against Simon, but Peter is a rock and a big threat to him. He cannot prevail against Peter. Can heaven bank on your identity also? Can heaven predict you? Can God say that He knows you and that you will not yield to the deceit of the enemy? There is something heaven is looking for in your curriculum vitae: it is your faithfulness, your ability to remain steadfast unto the end. God is not looking for the physical attributes that men are looking for. If heaven must enlist you in this recruitment exercise, it has to be by the Spirit of God.

"Upon this rock I will build my church." What Jesus means here is that He would build His church upon the Rock- the mystery that was revealed through Peter. He is also saying here that Peter could be the set man or the presiding exemplary head of the kind of church He wanted to build. That is, leaders that can connect and download the mind of God per time. This also reveals to us that the church of Jesus must be founded only on revelation, not information and must continue to be built on revelation.

Jesus must have been happy to have called Peter blessed. Peter's response was the evidence that His work on earth would have a great foundation and be fruitful. The last part of the verse also makes it clear to us that it is only the Ekklesia, which is built on the Rock (Revelation) that can survive the crises of this world.

In verse 19, Jesus made another profound statement: And I will give you the keys of the kingdom of Heaven. Whatever you forbid (bind or lock) on earth will be forbidden in heaven and what you permit (loose or open) on earth will be permitted in heaven.

It is important that we bear in mind that we are called to operate as citizens of the kingdom not as a church (denomination). We are members of an assembly for a specific reason. For instance, a member of a senate may be addressed as a senator. That is just part of his identity, but he is still a citizen of a country. That's exactly what the church is. The kingdom is higher than church. The church is just a part of God's kingdom. God's kingdom is not just heaven. Heaven also is just a part of the kingdom. The kingdom of God is very vast and dynamic. The Bible says we are the light of the world, not the light of the church; light cannot express itself in the church. It has to shine through the darkness of the world. It is sad that the Church today has so many lights trying to outshine one another, whereas the world is full of darkness. If you as a believer will show forth your light at your place of work, then you will become more relevant.

Revelation is the only thing that can unlock the keys of the kingdom of heaven. Remember, it is not just a "key" but "keys." This means that no religious and theological formula can get you things from the store of heaven except by revelation. You cannot get results by simply maintaining the status quo. That would be tradition. The fact that you got something done in a particular way for God does not mean it should become a permanent formula; you have to inquire of God through the Spirit continuously. This also implies that what was called a revelation yesterday can become a mere information or tradition today. David was called a man after God's own heart because he always inquired of God before he took any step. This is how God expects us to walk if we are going to be successful with Him.

The fact that there are many keys tells us that one formula can't open every door. There is only one God, but there are many keys for different things we need on earth: good marriage, finances, good health, achievement and accomplishment, breakthrough, etc. All these things cannot be opened with one key. To some, absolute obedience to the command of God is what will bring results; to some, it is prayer and fasting; to some, worship; to some, giving and to some, faith. The reason many are struggling is that they are not making use of the right key. Getting things done must be by revelation, not just by practicing religion.

Religion is to have a form of godliness, but lacks the power of God.

Having keys also means having access to heavenly things. This means that regardless of your religious position or office, if you cannot touch heaven while on earth, you may likely not end up there someday. We must grow into maturity in the Spirit to a point where we can handle the keys of the kingdom from here on earth and make things happen. Whatever you forbid on earth is forbidden in heaven. When you are operating at this level, you can interface within two realms: the terrestrial and the celestial (Earth and Heaven). This was how we were originally created. The Bible records that God came down to the Garden of Eden at the cool of the day to interact with Adam and Eve. Ask yourself this question: Is God a man with flesh? The answer of course is "No!" Adam and Eve were created as spirits (in God's image) but they were designed with the capacity to relate perfectly with the Earth and Heaven at the same time. The operation of the Garden of Eden is a realm that the church has not yet been restored even with the sacrifice and resurrection of Jesus Christ. No wonder He says "I'll build my own kind of Ecclesia (church)"

I. This is to say that we determine the destiny of the earth, if only we can operate at this level

II. God cannot do anything on earth until we invite Him to do so.

III. We have power to kill and to make alive.

IV. This also means we are to be reverenced and absorbed on earth as kingdom citizens

Beloved, I don't know what particular "brand" of church you belong to, but my desire is that as you read on, you will be able to perfectly identify yourself with Jesus' kind of assembly (Ecclesia).

COMPARISON BETWEEN JESUS' CHURCH AND OTHERS

There are things that Jesus saw in the assembly of the Roman Government and the people of God (Old Testament), which had a different leadership style of a different generation; from the Moses' era to that of Joshua and to the days of the Scribes and the Pharisees. For the sake of time, we shall compare them juxtaposed, and as you read through this, consider with sincerity the side to which you belong.

A. The Roman Government assembly was established by constitutional law (Act 19:39-40). God also established the assembly of the Israelites in order to take them through the transition into grace by the reformation of their minds, but they enjoyed corruption (Deut. 9 10-12). None of the two examples cited above is perfect. Many churches today have promoted constitution so much that even the Holy Spirit cannot change their laid down rules, regulations and the operation. However, the church of Jesus is supposed to be flexible in the hand of the Holy Spirit, which is the Life of the church.

B. The assembly of the Romans and the Israelites were mainly ruled by intellectuals, mostly lawyers, who were versed in the constitutional provision. For instance, the Pharisees and the Scribes were teachers of the law. They represent the theologians and religious leaders of today who have so many degrees and whom men have approved because of their certificates and professional reputations. However, Jesus also had some intellectuals like Matthew and Luke in His assembly, although the majority of His disciples were not so educated. This shows us that it is not in the eloquence of speech or how versed a man is that qualifies him, but his understanding of spiritual things.

C. The members of the assemblies (Romans and Israelites) were very proud by virtue of their positions and birthright. Even today, majority of the Israelites are very conscious of their position in God by reason of the old covenant, calling themselves children of Abraham. But Jesus emphasized that even if we must boast at all; it should be in the things of the Spirit, that which expresses our true identity.

D. The Ekklesia of the Romans and the Israelites are mostly ruled by the final verdicts of the members, usually after series of hot arguments. Jesus' proposed assembly is to be built only on revelation.

E. The Romans' and Israelites' assemblies did not have the capacity to relate with the things of God freely; they only practiced religion, which was more of a carnal form of worship. The church of Jesus, however, has worshippers who worship God in spirit and in truth.

God is hereby opening our eyes to see the concerns of His heart so that we may know where we belong. I will suggest that you continue in the spirit of prayer as we move ahead in this journey together. What you are reading will not just be another ordinary book, but rather, your life will encounter the Spirit of truth and revelation, and the Spirit of God will illuminate your heart and bring about a reformation in your soul.

Chapter 4

Jesus' Pattern For Church Building

"David did not win any of his battles because he was a professional; he won because he was prophetical. My greatest desire is to understand the mind of God per time"

"Don't be ridiculous!" Saul replied, "There's no way you can fight this Philistine and possibly win! You're only a boy, and he's been a man of war since his youth..." "I can't go in these," (Saul armor of war) he protest to Saul. "I'm not used to them" so David took off again.
1 Samuel 17:33&39b

The church of Jesus Christ is absolutely different from religious assemblies in identity, structure and potency because of the process it had to go through. We shall consider the nature of the processes one after the other.

I WILL BUILD MY CHURCH II

In the past chapters, we tried to define the true meaning of the word church and its origin. We came to a conclusion that the original Greek meaning of church is Ekklesia, which by interpretation means "assembly" or "called out." We also looked at other types of assemblies that were called out for other purposes. We compared different assemblies and their features and we also checked the principles behind the Jesus' declaration, "I will build my church.

At this juncture, we will be making use of the words "assembly" or "called out" interchangeably in place of the word "church" as the case may be.

In the history of the world, before Jesus declared his own concept of the church, the phrase "Building church" had never been used. Don't forget that "churches" had been before Christ, but those ones came to be by democracy and other systems of government inaugurated by law, not by building. Jesus' declaration of building His own church was a strange language in those days. This was because the church He proposed to build was a living one, comprising of people (I Corinthians 13:9). It does not make much sense to say you are going to build human beings.

Jesus' movement also came with other terms and new waves of frequency which the existing assemblies and even the world couldn't decode. The gap between the Jesus mindset (technologies) and others was far beyond the difference between Analogue and Digital operations.

The concept of the church from Jesus' point of view negates the popular view of the world. For instance, in John 2: 17-20, the Jewish leaders demanded from Him the sign and evidence that His authority was from God. He replied, "All right, destroy this temple and in three days I will raise it up" (verse 17). "What!" They exclaimed. "It took forty-sixty years to build this temple, and how can you rebuild it in three days?" But when Jesus said "This temple," He actually referred to His own body (Verse 19-21). Of course, we may not be able to blame these leaders, because to them the temple was just a physical building that men labour to construct. In their own understanding, it had nothing to do with humans, but where people only gather to worship.

THE GREAT SHIFT

Whenever there is a new move of God on earth, what it implies is that there has been a shift in the spirit. It means that the status quo is no more the same and a brand new technology has been introduced to take the kingdom of God to the next level. And anytime this happens, we will begin to see God raising pioneers of this new move, declaring God's message for the time as the Spirit grants them utterance. Secondly, deeper revelations will begin to enter into the hearts of men through the Holy Spirit. We saw an example in the book of Acts, on the day of Pentecost. Another reality is that Jesus' language and expressions defied the rules of the language of His time. This is why it will be very difficult for a rigid man to move or shift with the move of God. When Jesus began to introduce the message of the kingdom, the Pharisees, who had been beneficiaries of the old pattern, saw the new move as a threat to their own personal agenda. They found it difficult to accept His message because they thought it could make their own religion of no effect, taking the attention of the people from them and fixing it on God and the kingdom.

Beloved, let us not lose sight of the fact that in the eyes of the public, Jesus was either John the Baptist, Elijah, Jeremiah or one of the old prophets (Matthew 16:14). These were some of the great men the people were used to. They were men whom God had used to declare the new move that was going to come so that the people could prepare their hearts, although they themselves had limits. These ancient prophets did not have that capacity to move the men of their days into the new dispensation that they spoke about because the time of manifestation had not yet come. There is a popular saying that change is the only constant thing in life. Even the model of modern technology of our world has continued to change at a rapid rate. All these things are also applicable in the spirit realm. The scripture has revealed that in the last days, the knowledge of the glory of the Lord will cover the earth as the waters cover the sea. This further reveals to us that a rigid man cannot walk with God. If God starts with you and you refuse to move when heaven has already moved, you will soon be abandoned and become obsolete like the Pharisees who refused to key into the move of God through Jesus Christ.

Register this in your mind today that the move of God is not stagnant. God is dynamic. He is taking the church from one level of glory to another and He will not stop until the church gets to the final destination. Finishing strong goes beyond being consistent with the things you started many years ago. It is not compulsory that you continue with the same pattern or style. David inquired from God at all times; he did not base his walk with God on experience. It is too dangerous to get used to God's ways and style, because you might end up being where He used to be and not where He is. As long as shifting continues in the spirit, God is still building and He will not stop until we finally get to our destination- where we will not be different from Jesus Christ any longer.

BUILDING ON THE ROCK (The Platform)

A builder considers two major things while planning to build. Firstly, he considers the kind of structure he wants to build and secondly, he considers the kind of soil texture for the structure he wants to build. Sometimes, many tests will be carried out to identify the soil type and the solidity of the ground in order to determine the kind of structure that should be on it. Jesus was very wise to have considered building on the rock. He said. "Upon this rock I will build my church, and the power of hell will not conquer it."

In ancient times, the mountains were used by men for refuge whenever there was war. Those cities that were also built on the hills usually found it easier to launch attacks faster and better because they could easily see their enemies from afar. This explains why it is safer to build on the rock than on the sand. Hear what David says:

"The Lord is my rock, my fortress, and my Saviour. My God is my rock, in whom I find protection. He is my shield", the power that saves me, and my place of safety. He is my refuge, my Saviour, the one who saves me from violence." 2 Samuel 22:3

Beloved, can you see the understanding and the revelation that made David stand out in his time? Can you now see why God called him a man after His own heart? He said, "The Lord is my fortress and my mighty rock where I hide." This was the song David sang to the Lord on the day he was delivered from his enemies and from Saul. Jesus was very emphatic when He said that the gates of hell (the total conclusion, decision and delusion from the kingdom of darkness) will not pollute or defile the church He would build on the rock powerless. This implies that there can never be a true church without constant revelation from God. When there is no constant revelation, the church will just be like every other organization, having wonderful structures and following after protocols. It doesn't matter how many thousands of people at church has been able to draw to itself, if it is not founded on the rock, which is revealed, it will fall.

Revelation brings light and refreshing to man. Without it, there will be dryness. When a man jumps out of God's revelation, he will begin to quote statistics, psychology and information that strengthen the soul and weaken the spirit. Your spirit can only receive life through revelation. When a man is void of revelation (prophetic direction and instruction) from God, it is just a function of time; the gates of hell will conquer what he is building.

On two occasions God asked Moses to go to the rock with the elders of the children of Israel to bring water out of it. The first time, He asked Him to smite the rock but the second time, He asked him to speak to it (Exodus 17:1-7, Numbers 20:2-3). God wanted the elders to recognize Him as their source; that was why He didn't want Moses to use the same method twice. He did not want the children of Israel to idolize the rod of Moses that brought out water from the rock. Already, God was gradually taking the Israelites on a journey through which He would gradually knock out the system of Egypt that was already a part of them. He could not continue with Moses because he was too compassionate to get things done for Him. Moses began to lose the details that mattered to Him; he could no longer understand that things had been shifted in the spirit, and it was the same zeal that led to his death. Today, the major reason many people get written off by heaven is that they do not understand the present move of God. Though it may seem like they are still "pulling waves," it is a function of time, you will get to know that they have been obsolete or expired for so long. What you see as "revelation" is nothing but stale news as far as heaven is concerned. We need to be like the men of Isaachar who understood the times and seasons. (1 Chronicles 12:32).

The Israelites always got refreshed whenever they drank water from the rock. You may wonder why they drank from no other source except a rock. You may also wonder why God decided to make it happen in the presence of the elders. There is an adage that says, "A stream or river that forgets its source will soon dry up." "The Rock" is the source of revelation which is the only antidote for dryness. This proves to us that the slogan, "experience is the best teacher" is only the thought of a carnal mind. If experience is the best teacher Saul, with all his expertise in the art of warfare, would have easily defeated Goliath. The Bible tells us that it is the Holy Spirit who will teach us all things. Everything excludes nothing. Experience may handle newness of things or innovations, but it is only the Holy Spirit that can give you ideas that will change the course of your life, business, marriage, career and ministry. (John 14:26);

God spoke to me at a time and I heard it so clearly. He said, "Son, if only you will continue to let your life be guided by revelation, you will soon become a global success; it is only a function of time. Revelation from God will not always be something popular, but the truth is that it always stands the test of time and prevails in the end.

BUILDING WITH ROCK (THE STRUCTURE)

A rock can be defined as hard, solid material that forms part of the surface of the earth and other planets. It is in different shapes. There are three main types of it- volcanic, igneous and sedimentary rocks. Stone is a smaller version of it.

Jesus' emphasis on "rock" did not end on the platform of the church He proposed to build, but also on the laying of the structure. Earlier on, we defined "rock" as a revelation of God.

This implies that Jesus cannot lay a foundation on revelation and then build information or tradition on it. If that should happen the gates of hell will definitely prevail. The thoughts and imaginations of man's heart, which the bible describes to be evil, cannot be used to build the Church of God.

The fact remains that a house or structure can be built with bricks or stones. The houses built with stones are more expensive, durable, valuable, etc. than those with grass, wood or bricks. Stones typify the operations of the spirit while bricks typify the flesh and carnality. The Bible describes the temple of Solomon as built and repaired with stones, not bricks, grass or wood.

"The complex was three stories high, the bottom floor being 7½ feet wide, the rooms were connected to the walls of the temple by beams resting on the edges built out from the wall. So the beams were not inserted into the walls themselves. The stones used in the construction of the temple finished at the quarry, so there was no sound of hammer, axe, or any other iron tool at the building site." 1Kings 6:6-7

"Then they used the money for the construction Supervisions, which they used to pay the people working on the Lord's temple the carpenters, the builders, the masons, and the Stone Cutter. They also used the money to buy the timber and the finished stone needed for repairing the Lord's temple and they paid other expenses related to the temple's restoration." II King 12:11-12

Till date, the foundation of Solomon's temple can still be traced and people usually travel to Jerusalem from all over the world to see it. That is because it had a good foundation and the structure was made of solid stones. The Bible refers to Jesus also as a stone. David prophesied concerning Him, saying, "The stone that the builder rejected has now become the cornerstone." (Psalm 118:22). Jesus himself quoted exactly from the book of

Psalms (see Matt. 22:42, Mark 12:10). A cornerstone is not just any kind of stone, but a very strategic stone in a building, which if not properly placed, would result in the entire structure collapsing.

Any structure that will have eternal value must be built on the rock, which is revelation from God. Building on the rock entails starting off with God, building with the right pattern and materials and continuing in the same manner till the end. It is very possible for a man to start working with God and be faithful and consistent, even when fame, money and financial stability come. The Bible shows us in II Kings 12:11-12 that even repairs of the temple of Solomon were done only with stones, not bricks. Bricks may be easier to work with and cheaper compared to stones, but they do have eternal value; they are temporary materials. The Bible says our works shall be tested with fire (1 Corinthians 3:13-15). Beloved, examine yourself. Will your works remain or will they be consumed when tested by fire? We are all spirit beings and God expects that everything concerning our lives should be built on spiritual principles, not on popular opinion or the things we think are in vogue.

Chapter 5

The Bricks Versus The Stones

"Anybody can build, but building a lasting super structure that will impact my world with a relevant and seasoned resource continuously is my challenge."

"For we are both God's workers, and you are God's field. You are God's building... Because of God's grace to me, I have laid the foundation like an expert builder. Now others are building on it. But whoever is building on this foundation must be very careful."
1 Corinthians 3:9-10

There were several instances in the scriptures where individuals, groups of people and nations set out to build notable structures. Noah, for example, was commanded by God to build an ark; Moses was instructed to build a tabernacle while Solomon was asked to build a temple. There were also some people who desired to build structures, contrary to the will of God. A good example is found in Genesis 11, where the people of Babylonia desired to build a tower to the height of heaven. We shall observe how these people built and the materials they build with and then compare their pattern with that of our Lord Jesus.

At one time all the people of the world spoke the same language and used the same words. As the people migrated to the east; they found a plain in the Land of Babylonia and settled there. They began saying to each other "Let's make bricks and harden them with fire." (In this region bricks were used instead of stone, and tar was used for mortar). Then they said "come, let's build a great city for ourselves with a tower that reaches into the sky (heaven). This will make us famous and keep us from being scattered all over the world." But the Lord came down to look at the city and the towers the people were building. "Look!" He said, "The people are united, and they all speak the same language. After this, nothing they set out to do will be impossible for them! Come, let's go down and confuse the people with different languages. Then they won't be able to understand each other." In that way, the Lord scattered them all over the world, and they stopped building the city. Genesis11:1-8

In Building Engineering, most of the work that involves the use of stones can also be done using bricks, depending on how solid the bricks or the concrete is. The fact, however, is that bricks and stones do not have the same durability and value. A land value, usually does more of an internal than external examination when trying to determine the monetary value of a building. Jesus also emphasized the fact that our works shall be tested. It means that no matter how beautiful our works are from afar, what actually matter most are the materials, which they are made of. It also implies that the church today was designed long ago by Jesus and the pattern and materials involved in the building was described without provision for an alternative. The church must either be built to conform to Jesus' pattern otherwise it will conform to the Babylonian pattern- the system of this world, which represents the operations of the kingdom of darkness. It is not enough to have the zeal to build for God. One must build according to His laid down principles and patterns. We would analyze both Jesus' pattern, which is Zion and the Babylonia pattern. We will examine the principles and the materials involved in these two kingdoms and see how they differ.

Looking through the scriptures from Genesis 11 to Revelations, we would see that in principles and operations Babylon is described as oppressive, manipulative, enslaving, selfish, intimidating and self-aggravating. It encompasses every part of the existing sector of today's world system. Babylon is not just a location; it is a system of operation. You find the Babylonian system in industries, businesses and governments. Unfortunately, this system is waxing stronger in the churches today. It is an anti-Zion system that promotes man rather than God.

WHICH SYSTEM CONTROLS YOUR OPERATIONS?

Beloved, pride and ignorance are part of the greatest weapons of the enemy against the church of God in these last days. The fact that you have what Babylonia system describes as a success by her parameter does not mean it is success from God's perspective. The emphasis on the spirit now is not just success, but fulfillment, which can only be measured by God. Whatever you are building must align with the purpose and exact plans of God for your life. Everything you are building must be according to the measurement God requires from you. He gave Noah the exact measurements He wanted for the ark. He even described the kind of wood he should use. For the Solomon's temple, He also gave precise details of how it should be built (1 Kings 6). Beloved, I have a great burden and concern for the body of Christ. It causes me deep pain and tears. I pray that the eyes of our understanding will be opened the more. Are you aware that a lot of work will be burnt by fire as the Bible says in I Corinthians 3:13-15. It doesn't matter how beautiful what you have built so far may be; it doesn't matter the cost involved or the crowd it has attracted; if it is not the exact picture of what God has designed for you then you have to quit building. It doesn't matter how far you've gone, you can still make a "U" turn and switch to God's pattern and say farewell to Babylon.

Can you remember the last time you cross- checked the blueprint of God for your life? When was the last time you stopped to consider what you are building? Have you ever asked yourself: Whose parameter am I using to build? Who am I taking as a standard for my life, ministry, marriage and business? Whom have I called to direct my building process? Who really committed this work into my hands? Who am I accountable to? Beloved, let your heart be open today. God is not moved by how much crowd you have been able to gather. There is a speed mentality that has hit the church today and that is making her to gather both goats and sheep together. Many are looking for popularity and large congregation without any kingdom value that can impact the world.

The truth remains that every man will stand before the throne of God to give an account of his work here on earth. Apostle Paul was sent to the Gentiles while Peter was sent to the Jews. The Bible says that He gave to every man grace according to his capacity and assignment. Have you realized that your assignment here on earth is not by your decision but by discovery? If truly it is by discovery, how come you are copying someone else in building what God has given you to build?

This is one problem I have with people that are used to a particular number of keys and points for success in business, marriage or ministry. As much as information is good, revelation is better. You cannot continue to read the same books, attend the same conferences, apply the same principles and still expect to get different results. You have leaned on information for so long. Information could either be an idea from the soul or an expired revelation (old order). There is, however the fresh word and the divine information. It is called revelation. That is what heaven wants to make known to you today. It is the only thing that can set you above others.

Studying the life of Jesus, one would discover that He was 100 percent God and 100 percent man when He was on earth. He said: "I tell you the truth, the Son can do nothing by Himself. He does only what He sees the Father do. Whatever the Father does the Son also does" (John 5:19). Who are you then to absolutely depend on yourself and on the advice of mentors to build what God has called you for? I am not saying that having a mentor is bad, but you need to strike a balance and define your limit, recognizing that God is the One who has the final authority over you and your work. He is the One to whom you will submit your building reports and balance sheets. You must therefore be careful how you build. Remember this: you are building not to please men, but to please God. He owns the work and He has thought it wise to graciously appoint you to build for Him, so build according to His pattern and specifications alone.

BABYLON VERSUS ZION'S OPERATION

There is a need for us to have a clear picture of what the Babylonian system called deception is all about. It represents everything that is anti-God in its operation. We shall consider the operations of Zion too. These two operations can easily be categorized under two systems: BRICKS and STONES.

Each of these systems has its own methods of operations. We shall get a better understanding by using Bricks and Stones as the principal materials in building each system. We would need to go through Genesis 11:1-8 again to first understand the dimensions of Babylon.

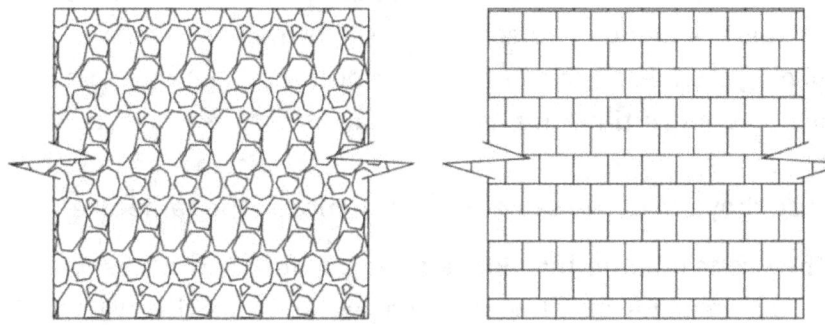

Fig A: Building or structure with stone (unequal shapes and sizes)

Fig. B: Building of structure with bricks (equal shapes and sizes)

THE PRINCIPLES OF BABYLON (BRICKS)

The whole world was speaking the same language at this point in time, which was a strength and energy for community works, therefore they decided to live together and found a plain land in Babylon. The Babylonians chose a convenient place for themselves- a plain land not a rocky place and neither a valley. This implies that they chose a comfort-zone. The Bible declares,

"Woe unto them that are ease in Zion." This means that in Zion you are neither living for yourself nor for comfort, but for the will and pleasure of the Father. They began to consult with each other, on chosen bricks instead of stones.

Bricks are ideas of men (man-made) whereas stone is a technology from God (blue- print of the Spirit). Bricks have a molding formula (a constructed or designed shape that brings the exact figure) according to the size designed by man, while stones are of different shapes (purposes in a singular will of God). The bricks look alike because they are patterned after a particular mode - a symbol of limitation, competition and repetition, but every stone is unique, either in size or shape (divine revelation to individuals are uniquely released by God). Bricks are easier to use in building compared to the stones of different shapes and sizes. Stones take more time to position if the structure would be well built. Bricks, on the other hand, can easily stand on another because they are of the same shape and mostly the same size.

They concluded in building a great city for themselves with a tower that reaches into the sky (heaven) and said this will make us famous on earth. Genesis 11:4

The motive of this people was wrong from the outset. We do not exist for ourselves but for God. This is the formula for success. However, the principles that Babylon is teaching are already being peddled in the church today. Your primary reasons for living and going into ministry should not be to have the biggest ministry or become the richest person in the land. It is to give pleasure to God by building according to His dictate.

What is the reason behind your pioneering work today? Be very sincere with God and with yourself. What are the motives and ideas that led to this? You can pull it down or bring an end to it if the intentions are wrong or not in line with God's purpose for your life. This reminds me of the question I asked my lady friend some times ago: "What would happen, assuming we do not acquire the things that men have set as a standard for measuring success in ministry such as cars, beautiful architectural masterpiece and other good things of life while doing the will of God?" I needed to know before our relationship gets deeper and culminates in marriage. Just like the three Hebrew boys who were threatened with a fiery furnace if they fail to worship the golden image erected by Nebuchadnezzar's men, I am not ready to change my mind or to compromise God's standard for any mundane thing. The people who were building the tower of Babel also wanted to live together contrary to the will of God. They were not ready to take responsibility for their world. We are called to be the light of the world, not the assembly (church). Why do we all sit down in the assembly without taking good decisions that would benefit our world and the purpose of God on earth. They desired to be famous on earth. This portrays what Babylonian churches are pursuing. Television and Radio today are given special priority for different motives. No man can judge your motive, but you must ask yourself certain crucial questions. This will determine the results you will get. What is the motive behind your style? Is it to bring glory to yourself or God? It is left to you to answer for yourself.

In verse 5, God saw that they could not be stopped from carrying out their intentions because they were united in language. This implies that the multitude agreeing with you on what you are doing or building does not necessarily mean it is of God. Things may look good and yet not be of God. The truth however is that if it is not of God, it cannot be good regardless of your perspective about it. Do not be deceived to think that the majority always carries the vote or that the voice of men is the voice of God. Only one with God is a majority.

In verses 6 and 7, we see that there is power in agreement, whether positive or negative. These people were united; they were made in God's image so they understood the principle of oneness, although they used it negatively. No man could interrupt them except God. Unity of purpose is something the church need to get right in order to advance the kingdom. Building the church is beyond a one-man show mentality. Collective agreement, anointing, intercession and coercive responsibility are required if we are going to take the battle to the gates of the enemy.

In verse7 God said, "Come, let us go down and confuse the people with different languages. Then they won't be able to understand each other." It shows there is power in agreement. We ought to learn from the principle of praying in agreement. It is not the number of people praying that matters, but those in agreement. We can also make it our prayer point to set confusion in the camp of the enemies so that their language will not be one. The power of agreement lies in having the same language (mindset).

Differences between Bricks and Stone, typifying Babylon and Zion

	Bricks	Stones
1	Traditional operation from the souls of men.	Revelation from the heart of God.
2	Operations are often the same.	Dynamic because they are based on revelation.
3	Dismountable and can only last within a time frame. They are temporary.	They last longer and even outlive the builder and still stands.
4	It takes a profession to design bricks.	It takes the prophetic to receive and interpret revelation.
5	It is the work of the flesh (sensual).	It is the work of the Spirit.
6	It is easier to build with bricks.	It could be challenging to build with stones but always the best.
7	They are set in a particular order.	They cannot be set in a particular order but according to their shapes and sizes.
8	Anybody can imitate and duplicate a brick's ideology.	If it is a stone (revelation) it can't be exactly the same.
9	It can be imitated and pirated	It comes only by revelation.

Babylon (bricks) and Zion the (stones) are both spiritual dimensions that have physical expressions. Every operation, business, ministry or organization on the face of the earth falls under any of these two dimensions. You cannot be on the fence. You need to define the dimension you want to pattern your life after. Moreover, it doesn't matter how far you've gone on the journey. Pause for a minute and do a sincere self-examination. Carefully evaluate your life and everything you are building on earth. Are you pioneering a Babylonian system or movement? Go back to the comparison table of the bricks and stones. I pray that the Holy Spirit will reveal Himself to you and you would be humble enough by the power of God to take corrections.

First of all, what is your source of inspiration? Pause and think. Why are you doing or ready to do what you have proposed to do? Are you moved by what you drive or what drives you? Can you boldly say that what you are pursuing is a vision (from God) or Ambition (men's desires)? Don't be deceived, two men may be pursuing a singular objective and one can be a vision while the other can be an ambitious. It doesn't matter the color or embellishments you apply to what you are building, God sees all your motives and intentions.

What school of thought do you belong? Are you professionally driven or prophetically driven? David did not win Goliath because he was professionally trained, but because he was prophetically tutored (understanding the mind of God). Saul couldn't achieve this great feat with his trained army and weapons of war. The only thing the devil does not understand is revelation. That is why God wants believers to operate by revelation in every issue that concerns them. You cannot suffer loss in business if you understand the mind of God on time. He will tell you things that professional investment analysts cannot dabble into. Is intelligence your most esteemed value or are you driven by integrity? Revelation will place you above others while tradition, repetition, competition and information will place you either below or on the average. Revelation makes you see ahead of time and causes you to understand times and seasons of life. You can only get this by connecting to God through the Holy Spirit. Trying to find a short cut to your destiny can cut you short. Go for God through revelations even when it seems it is no more in vogue; it is always the best. God alone can reveal timeless truths.

Today, internet information is gradually replacing revelation in the body of Christ, especially among new generation ministers of the gospel. The Bible says, "A man shall not live by bread alone, but by every word that is released from the mouth of God" (Luke 4:4). This means that just as bread gives you the physical energy, divine revelation on a daily basis is the only thing that can sustain life. The 'every word' here is beyond just reading of scripture, but receiving of instruction, rebukes, direction and inspiration from the Holy Ghost through the reading of the word. If you read the Bible everyday without getting revelation from the Holy Spirit, you will just end up storing history in your head. The scripture contains both the letter and the spirit. The letter kills, but the Spirit gives life. Request for the inspiration of the Spirit on a daily basis as you study the word.

Chapter 6

The Church And The Gates of Hell

"A man's success is not determined by the size of his personal achievements, but by the measure of his impact on his world."

"God's purpose in all this was to use the church to display his wisdom in its rich variety to all the unseen rulers and authorities in the heavenly places."
Ephesians 3:10

Before we proceed further in this chapter, there is a need for us to do a recap of the things we have said earlier. We have been able to establish that the word church originally came from the word Ekklesia and connotes:' assembly or 'called out'. We have also looked at the components and the competence of the church Jesus is building on this earth. Jesus is building a brand of church that will take charge of the global constituency without being defined by geographical location. This Jesus' kind of Church will never be overcome by the prince of this world and his entire kingdom.

WHAT ARE THE GATES OF HELL?

There are two key words in the above question: gates and hell. If we can have a deeper understanding of what each of them means, then we need to have a clear picture of what "the gates of Hell" means, and also what Jesus was talking about when referring to this phrase in his statement "….and the gates of hell shall not prevail against it." (KJV)

WHAT IS HELL?

Throughout the scriptures, hell is not for once described as a good place. It is described as a bottomless pit; a place designed for the devil and his angels, a place of darkness, a domain or assembly of the wicked and the rebellious, including the devil their master. (See II Peter 2:4, Deut 32:22, Rev. 17:8).

WHAT ARE GATES?

A gate can be described as an entry point. Gates are often placed between fences and they can be opened or closed. However, the dimensions of gates that Jesus was referring to are mysterious channels through which access is given to entities without any physical restrictions or barriers. These gates are more spiritual than physical. This was the dimension of gates David also saw in Psalm 24.

Open up, ancient gates! Open up, ancient doors, and let the King of glory enter. Who is this King of glory? The LORD, strong and mighty; the LORD, invincible in battle. Open up, ancient gates! Open up, ancient doors, and let the King of glory enter. Who is the King of glory? The Lord of Heaven's Armies He is the King of glory. (Psalm 24:7-10)

A lot of things happened between the period of Jesus' death and resurrection. He descended to hell to defeat and disarm the powers of darkness and to set the captives free. After He arose from the grave, He declared, "All power in heaven and earth, even under the earth has been given to me." David got the revelation about the revolting of hell against the King of kings, the Lord of lords, the Maker of everything, including the hell and its hosts. God can't be hindered. (Isaiah 45:2-3). The eyes of your understanding must be opened. Can you imagine hell protesting against the entering of the Lord into its domain by shutting the gates? It acknowledged the implication of His visit that it would not just be to set men free, but to also declare that all power belongs to God. Scriptures say that He also collected the keys of death and hell. (Rev 1:18, Rev 6:8). Therefore, death should not be a threat to the church any longer if we truly know that the devil does not have this power again. Death can only overcome us if we give the power to the devil through our ignorance. In summary, the second dimension of gates is a realm, whereby the devil locked up rights, opportunities, dominion and resources of men as long as there is no intervention by a greater power.

THE THIRD DIMENSION OF GATES

We have established that the first dimension of gates is the mere entry point into a geographical territory and that the second dimension is a spiritual entry point into a particular realm in the spirit. The third dimension of the gates could be defined as a congregation of rulers, authorities and decision makers.

Jesus knew what He meant when He said. "... the gates of hell shall not prevail." There is nothing that takes place in the physical that has not first taken place in the spiritual realm. For instance, when you see a man that starts misbehaving in marriage, or at office, contrary to his personality, you should know that he is being manipulated from the pit of hell and a negative decision has been made against him too. It also signals that at a particular time, that you may not even be aware that such a man (victim) might have compromised or be disconnected from the source (God). When you see a particular trait so prevalent within a particular ethnic group, cultures, races or nations, believe me, negative decision and manipulation have been programmed against them. Let us look at one more scripture to establish this truth and revelation about the third dimension of the gates. Proverbs 31:10-23 describes the quality of a wife who is of a noble character- a virtuous woman. Verse 23 describes her husband: Her husband is well known at the city gates, where he sits with other civic leaders." The KJV says, "Her husband is known in the gates, when he sitteth among the elders of the land."

From the scripture above, we can see vividly that the gate is a place of higher authority in the land. It is where the elders often sit. When we talk about "gates," we are referring to different sets of decision makers. In the realm of the spirit of darkness, there are many gates: witches and wizards, the occult, the marine kingdom and deceptive religious and traditional practitioners all over the world. It may surprise you to know that although these agents of darkness are many, when it comes to making decisions over the destinies of nations and communities, they do not disagree. This is because they are working for the cause of their master, the devil. You will now see why many kings and traditional rulers are usually initiated into different cults and secret societies before they are able to assume office in any community or region. There are gates through which the decisions and influence from the kingdom of darkness enter into our cities.

Oftentimes whenever I go for mission outreaches and I see missionaries working in ignorance, my heart bleeds. God says, "My people are destroyed because of lack of knowledge." This knowledge goes beyond knowing how to preach or endure hardship on the field; it is revelation knowledge on how to handle issues and operations in those territories that matters. Many zealous missionaries have become casualties, losing their lives, marriages, and their children to attacks from the enemy. Many do not have a full prophetic understanding of the gates within their territories and how to overcome them. I urge and beseech you by the mercies of God to take praying for missionaries on the field as a responsibility. Ask God to empower them the more and to open their eyes of understanding so that they would know how to handle the gates of hell over their cities and communities. There are two things you need to take note of here: it is either these missionaries conquer the gates of the community they are residing in or the gates conquer them. Jesus made it known that the gates of hell shall never conquer the church He's building. This means that the devil has succeeded in afflicting the church with ignorance.

THE COMBINED OPERATION OF THE THREE DIMENSIONS OF GATES

The first dimension we point out as the physical gates of the cities and nations are contact points to the spirit. Note that no spirit can work on earth except there is an entity they can work with. Such entity includes witches and wizards. They operate through women and men, respectively. A man will still remain a normal human until he carries that spirit that take charge and total control of him.

When a decision is taken in the third dimension at the seat of judgment where there is approval or authority of cases concerning men and his environment, the second dimension is contacted for keeping of files, records, virtues of lives, national destinies, etc. The second dimension (grave) is one of the largest storage departments of the hell. It was to this second dimension that Jesus went to collect the keys of death and hell that the devil held on to against humanity and nations. It was to this action of Jesus that brought out a prophetic declaration and conversation: "lift up your heads, O ye gates and be ye lift up, ye everlasting doors; and the King of glory shall come in. Who is this King of glory? The LORD strong and mighty, the LORD mighty in battle" (Psalm 24:7-8 KJV). This is not yet hell fire. Hell fire is reserved for the last judgment (See Matthew 18:9, 5:22). Don't mix them up; hell fire will start functioning after Jesus has finally judged the devil and his angels, so that they can be there (hell fire) forever and ever.

Have you ever asked yourself: why do men make sacrifices at the road-junctions in cities and villages? Who are they appeasing to if not the demonic powers that be? The destinies of cities are controlled and manipulated by gates; so also are the inhabitants. No spirit can operate on earth without having a human being to inhabit. When you see occult men, herbalists, and false prophets in the villages and cities, they are also doorways for demonic operations.

I feel you don't need to know so much about the devils operations, but to know more of God. He will reveal to you what you need to know about the operations of the demonic influences around you and even your territory and how to combat them.

One thing I know is that you need to trace these powers and influences by governmental prayers or prophetic prayers, declaring with boldness and authority as the one in charge. The spirit (devil) doesn't have any legal ground on the earth. The Bible says: "Ye are blessed of the Lord, which made heaven and earth. The heaven, even the heavens, are the LORD's but the earth has he given to the children of men." (Psalm 115:15-16 KJV). This Scripture would open our eyes of understanding as to whether a spirit which is of God or the devil can operate on earth without flesh (human or animal). When the devil is desperate of operating on earth sometimes, he can do so low through animals. But our God can only reside in the image He created for this singular purpose - man. Therefore, Jesus' declaration that the gates of hell shall not prevail is not a joke at all. It is a prophetic picture of the church He was about to build at that point of the declaration. And He knew that if truly His church would be built according to His designed pattern, it would be totally impossible for the gates of hell to prevail over it.

THE POSITION OF THE CHURCH OVER THE GATES OF HELL

Without any iota of doubt, you would agree with me that Jesus was not test- running the proposed church (assembly) that is far stronger than the gates of hell. As a matter of fact, His church was designed to deal with the devil, by teaching him and his angels the manifold wisdom and power of God, which is resident in us. At least for choosing to rebel against the order of our Father in heaven, the earth shouldn't have been a conducive place of operations for the devil if truly we are in charge as the mandate was given to us. This earth has been allocated to you and me to demonstrate the glory and dominion of our Father's kingdom. We should not negotiate the kingdom with the devil. (Read 1John 5:4-5, Eph. 3:10).

As ambassadors and kingdom citizens, we must not be eager or anxious to leave this world to "go to heaven" as many people desire. Our primary place of function, assignment and purpose is the earth. Our Father has chosen us to "kingdomise" the earth, such that it will be like heaven: Thy will be done on earth as it is in heaven. (Matthew 6:10)

Today, the church of Jesus has been wounded, has also sustained injuries, and is looking for deliverance meetings up and down. Ironically, the saints were originally built with software of absolute rulership and dominion. Unfortunately, the devil is using ignorance as a tool of destruction against men and making them to live below God's ordained standard. Our battle with the devil would be as tough as we promote it ignorantly. We are to declare our prophetic authority to the devil by revelation that he has no place here on earth. The disciples of our Lord Jesus came back with testimonies that demons were messed up in their apostolic mission work. To them that was the greatest achievement, but Jesus replied and made them realize that, this act was only part of the package. Whenever you take your place, the devil submits to you automatically. It is not by prayer alone, but also by right knowledge the devil gives up. The problem with the church is that we specialize in declaring religious authority. This can't work. The devil does not respect titles or positions. Where do you belong to in the Spirit? Is your name a threat to the devil? We were designed to be a great threat to the devil's kingdom like Jesus' name and Paul's. Read this and ponder: "A group of Jews was traveling from town to town casting out evil spirits. They tried to use the name of the Lord Jesus in their incantation, saying, "I command you in the name of Jesus, whom Paul preaches, to come out! Seven sons of Sceva, a leading priest, were doing this. But one time when they tried it, the evil spirit replied, "I know Jesus, and I know Paul, but who are you? Then the men with an evil spirit leaped on them, overpowered them, and attacked them with such violence that they fled from the house, naked and battered." (Act 19:13-16).

Dear brothers and sisters, do you really know the blunders a lot of ministers of the Gospel are committing ignorantly, while some have sustained great injury by operating with second hand revelation? They enjoy quoting other people, thinking it will be possible to cast out devils without having a personal encounter, a deeper relationship and revelation knowledge of Jesus. It wouldn't work that way; rather you would sustain both spiritual and physical injury. Do you realize that the seven sons of Sceva were sons of a high priest? These were men who felt that ministry work was honorable and lucrative. They were preaching with the name they had never identified with. Just a simple question asked by the demon possessed knocked them. The man possessed with the evil spirit made them to know that the names of Jesus and Paul are too dangerous; they are no go areas as far as their kingdom was concerned. But we don't know you guys in our kingdom (Acts 19:12-16). This simply implies that you guys are just deceiving yourselves; you are not a threat to our kingdom. We can't bow to your command, rather we would teach you guys a little lesson. "Immediately, they were beaten up. The Church of Jesus was designed to show the manifold wisdom of God (Ephesians 3:10).

Hello reader, are you still there? This is a great challenge for you and me. Our Lord Jesus is really disappointed in us. We are living like mere men. That is why many are sick and many are dying like mere men. We must rise up to our responsibilities and positions in God by activating the power, glory and the grace in the finished work Christ has done for us. Until this is done the true church will not emerge and the world will remain in confusion and in the midst of gross darkness. The church is the only light that can show the world the right direction, and the salt that can preserve the world for God in order to draw God's attention to the earth, thereby making the earth attractive and sweet for Him to come and dine (eat). One of our main functions as the salt of the earth is to sweeten the earth, this draws God's attention and we also preserve the earth from being corrupted as one of the abilities within us. You are the salt of the earth.

Chapter 7

The Church: God's Ambassadors

"The present state of the world is a true reflection of the state of the church."

"You are the salt of the earth. But what good is salt if it has lost its flavor? Can you make it salty again? It will be thrown out and trampled underfoot as worthless."
Matthew 5:13

One of the things I have come to understand in life is that a man can never perform or operate beyond his level of understanding of his position and his job description. For example, hiring a professional to work for you without giving him any job description will only amount to frustration at the end of the day. You will end up spending your time, money and other resources in vain. This means that you must first know exactly the problems you need able hands to fix.

I use the expression "able hands" because only a fool will discover a problem somewhere and just look for anybody to handle it. If men in their management positions will not make this mistake, we should not expect anything less from God. He has a mission and targets that is why He is looking for men and women that can represent Him fully in this generation.

God can use anybody but He will not use everybody. He can use anything but He will not use everything. First Peter 2:9 tells us that we are His chosen people. This simply means that He doesn't use everybody; He has certain yardsticks for choosing a selected few. That is why the Church is referred to as "the called out ones." No wonder the Scripture says we have been called out of the kingdom of darkness to the kingdom of His dear Son. One of the things the enemy desires to do is to rob us of this royal and ambassadorial identity, which makes us to be different from other men.

Jesus did not just come out with the church He didn't plan for. He had seen the future and even beyond this age. He therefore set a standard that would be able to withstand and survive in ages to come without being corrupted by the Babylonia system (the spirit of this world).

It is my earnest desire and prayer that the church of Jesus Christ (you and I) would walk in our true identity. Until this happens, we would continue to live like mere men and become vulnerable to the devil's attacks. This would also cause God to become disappointed in us and even our generation, to which we have been sent. Today we are getting so distracted by the flies that perch on us: our daily challenges and problems are gradually drawing our attention from our core purpose and assignment on earth. Our focus is now on ourselves rather than on the nations we have been set over. This is one of the strategies of the enemy to overcome us.

YOU ARE AN AMBASSADOR

Who is an ambassador? An ambassador is an executive officer who lives in a foreign country as a representative of his or her home country. Apostle Paul says, "So we are Christ's ambassadors; God is making His appeal through us" (II Corinthians 6:20). Do not forget that we are being built as a church by someone- Jesus Christ. Paul had this understanding, and he refers to the church as the ambassadors of Christ. An ambassador cannot resume in an office without proper understanding of his job, capabilities, privileges, rights and freedom of operation on behalf of his home country. An ambassador is the number one citizen of his own nation in any country, he has been assigned to. He has freedom of operation there as well as in his own country. He carries the full identity of his own nation. He is not governed by the laws of the nation he has been assigned to because he is not absolutely part of it. He works with time, because he knows he is not going to be in that nation forever. He takes full responsibility on behalf of his nation.

For instance, an American Ambassador or High Commissioner to any nation stands in the office of the American president to talk in that nation. Therefore, the people of the nation he has been assigned to cannot just ignore his words. In the same way, the identity of the church of Jesus on earth is so powerful and stronger than what any earthly ambassador possesses. Jesus said concerning the church He wanted to build on earth: "And I will give you the keys of the kingdom of Heaven. Whatever you forbid (bind or lock) on earth will be forbidden in heaven, and whatever you permit (loose, open or allow) on earth will be permitted in heaven." (Matthew 16:19).

The scripture above shows us that this particular class of ambassadors had never been on earth before. No wonder He said He would build His own brand of ambassadors- people who own the keys to solve diverse problems and challenges of the nations they have been sent to. Jesus' kind of ambassadors cannot be limited by the rules and systems of the world. Rather, they have the keys to get the world's problems solved. It does not matter the decisions made by the Governments of these nations, the ambassadors of Jesus can nullify them if they are not in line with the counsel of God.

In other words, the influence, power and authority vested on Jesus' ambassadors them him to be in charge of their home countries and the citizens of the foreign countries where they reside. Beloved, this had never been in the history of any kind of church. This is your real identity; you are the church. The Bible says you are an ambassador. It takes the active participation of all ambassadors to fully represent the interest of God's kingdom all over the earth. This means you are very important as an individual in the global agenda of God.

THE NATURE OF OUR ASSIGNMENT

Now that you have understood our relevance as ambassadors on earth (individually and collectively), we should understand that our existence and mandate are beyond us. We are no longer living for ourselves, but for the kingdom we are representing. We must deal with our personal challenges that could distract us from our core mission on earth. Remember, you did not send yourself to this nation you are presenting. The One who sent you provides even the life you are enjoying. This is what many motivational speakers do not understand and they thereby create so much confusion with their messages, trying to shift focus to themselves.

The fact that a person is an ambassador does not mean he would not experience the weather and encounter problems caused by some dysfunctions in the system of the nation where he has been assigned. On the other hand, experiencing these things does not also stop him from being an ambassador. The fact that you experience certain challenges in life does not in any way change you from being God's chosen representative. Do not allow the devil to take advantage of you by opening up the predicament of your life to you. The Bible says concerning Jesus that even though He was God's son, He learned obedience from the things he suffered (Hebrew 5:8). We all know Jesus as the Lord, but we see how He humbled Himself as a son of man. Did what He experienced on earth stop him from being God? The answer is "No!"

God is looking for the kind of church that will not compromise even in the midst of challenges and temptations, so that He can be effective and efficient in its operations on earth. These challenges are things that are associated with this world and they must not distract us. We should not forget that we were built with the software that can interface with two realms: heaven and earth. Whatever we forbid on earth is forbidden in heaven, and whatever we permit on earth will be permitted in heaven. Therefore, the challenges we face on earth are only positioned by the enemy to distract us from our goals, so that our minds could be focused on ourselves and the issues of the world instead of establishing the kingdom of God on the earth. Many of us hold the keys to the kingdom, but do not make proper use of them.

The truth is that ignorance kills. Purpose itself is life. The existence of a man becomes useless when purpose is not known. The Scripture says: 'The entire world is waiting earnestly for the manifestation of the sons of God" (Roman 8:19). Friends, as a global church, we are designed to bring glory to our King, by our operations and decisions on earth.

ACCOUNTABILITY OF THE AMBASSADORS

Every ambassador is placed on a particular geographical location (nation). There is an assignment you and I have been created for as individuals, and it is the executing of that assignment that can give us fulfillment in God. Imagine an ambassador in a foreign land pursuing nothing but his own personal ambition. There is a demand I see in the spirit now: it is called fulfillment. Align yourself to what you were created to do on earth (the nation(s) you were sent, not even what you see other ambassadors doing, because we all stand on different grounds before the same God who has appointed us as His ambassadors.

"Let a man so account of us as the ministers of Christ, and stewards of the mysteries of God. Moreover it is required in stewards that a man is found faithful" 1Corinthians 4:1-2 KJV

"I saw the dead, both great and small, standing before God's throne. And the books were opened, including the book of life. And the dead were judged according to what they had done, as recorded in the books" Revelation 20:12

"Look, I am coming soon, bringing my reward with me, to repay all people according to their deeds" Revelation 22:12

"For we must all stand before Christ to be judged. We will each receive whatever we deserve for the good or evil we have done in this earthly body" II Corinthians 5:10

Please, register this again in your heart: do not allow the zeal for what you are building and designing in the name of the Lord to get into your head or make you feel approved. Remember that you will give account of your jurisdiction and what you have done so far. It does not matter the extent or the volume of what you have done, if it is not in line with God's agenda and operational system, your labor is in vain. May this not be your portion! I am also careful in the way I am handling what God has committed to my hands, particularly in the writing of this book. I waited on the Holy Spirit before I wrote every chapter and also asked for what is in the mind of God for His church at this present time and season.

In Revelation 20:12, we read that many books were opened including the book of life, which contains the names of men and women who have been redeemed by the blood of Jesus. There are other books that contain the works of our hands and the operations of our hearts while we are here on earth. This implies that we will give an account of everything we do. It is also important to have a performance report as an ambassador. This is the understanding that the Apostle Paul had and enumerated in II Corinthians 5:10. He refused to be distracted by chains, imprisonments at all times, persecutions, intimidations, lack, people and religious leaders' opinions.

Beloved, the heart of Jesus is bleeding. He is saying, "Is this the church I built and died for?" His church has been distracted, pursuing shadows while the real thing is left untouched. It has lost its true identity, acquiring vain glory and honor to self, leaving the ministry of the saints to build personal empires, turning it to "Our church," defrauding God of His belongings, snatching the brides of Jesus- congregation- to themselves. The loyalty of the members is more to the set man than to Jesus, the Head of the church. They occupy the place of Jesus in people's heart, manipulating destinies by using the grace of God for personal enterprise. How do you build your marriage, God's holy institution? How do you raise your children? Is your lifestyle drawing people to Christ or is it sending them away from Him? Are you drawing people to your church just to increase membership or are you bringing them under the true lordship of Jesus, ensuring their hearts are set on Him? Heaven is reminding you today that the day of reckoning has been fixed. You will stand to give an account of your work. It is my prayer for you and me that our labor will not be in vain in the Lord.

THE CHURCH AND HER WORLD

We have seen the clear picture of Jesus' definition of the church, particularly His own brand. In another place, He described the church as the salt and the light of the world. He was accustomed to using the things that people were familiar with in their day-to-day activities to teach them spiritual lessons. Salt and light are very vital to the existence of humanity; therefore, using them to describe the church also shows how vital His church is to the world.

THE SALT OF THE EARTH

Apart from being an ingredient, another function of salt is that it preserves other ingredients. Jesus tried to use it to explain the relevance of the church to the world. The church must come to the understanding of this. Purpose is the essence of life. Living without purpose is equivalent to deadness. If the church does not understand its purpose, it will not function and therefore becomes dead. Jesus is saying that it is the presence of the church on the earth that is still making it (earth) to exist today. This means that there wouldn't have been any world without the church. The only reason God is still interested in the earth is that the church is still present.

In Genesis 18:16-33, God had made up His mind to wipe away the cities of Sodom and Gomorrah because of the gravity of their sins. However, He chose not to carry out His intentions without first consulting Abraham, a man who had a good relationship with Him. Abraham, then began to ask Him, saying, "Lord peradventure you find fifty righteous people living in these cities will you still wipe away the whole cities? God replied; if I can find fifty, I will spare the entire city for their sake."(Gen. 18:23-26). Abraham went on to ask God if he would spare the land if peradventure there were only forty-five righteous people there. He continued to bring the number down from the forty-five to forty, thirty, twenty and then ten (Genesis 18:27-32). God replied, "I will spare the city if I can just find ten righteous men in the land."

The church is the only preservative that God puts on earth. The presence of the church of Christ is what is preserving the nations of the world from decay and corruption. It is, however, unfortunate that the church is not only deviating from her primary functions, but is also getting corrupted by the system of the world. But one thing God keeps on emphasizing to me is that even the little disposed remnant on God's track will be equipped with the grace to do more and reproduce. Beloved, you need to ask yourself, "Of what importance am I to my world? "Can you say your presence in your family, organization and nation can preserve men and even an entire community from pollution through your exemplary lifestyle?" This goes beyond just praying for them to live in good health and not die. The usefulness of salt goes beyond sweetening or adding taste to food; it is also to preserve the food from getting spoilt on time. Life will be meaningless if it is not used to bring glory to God. The only way the church can make an impact on the earth is by having a positive influence on the lives of men.

THE SEASONING OF THE EARTH

Salt is one of the things that make food very delicious and appeal to the taste bud. As a matter of fact, it is the commonest food ingredient. Although it is not the most expensive, I would rather say it's the most important of all. Food will have no taste without it. We can therefore conclude that the Church, being the salt of the earth, does more than just the preservation of the earth. It also makes the earth, like food, appealing to God and even making Him to want to come down and dine (relate) with men on earth. If we are to enjoy the deeper presence of God on the earth, the way He came to relate to Adam and Eve in the cool of the day in the Garden of Eden, and the usual experience of Abraham who enjoyed a regular fellowship with Him, then we must stand to our responsibility. It was recorded that God came down on different occasions to discuss a heart to heart matters with Abraham. This means that our life and environment (communities and nation) must be made conducive for God to come and dine with us (Gen. 3:8-10; 18:17-23).

From the scriptures above, you will see that the relationship God had with Adam and Eve before their fall was superb. Genesis 3:8-10 reveals that Adam and Eve heard God walking in the garden even before calling them. This shows that was not their first experience with Him. He had been coming to them in a similar way to the extent that they were used to His footsteps. Abraham also had this experience (Gen 18:17, 22-23). What a fantastic relationship! This is what Christ called us to - "the called out ones" who have the capacity to relate with God in a mutual intimacy. As a matter of fact, the resurrection of Jesus brought us to a better and a higher level far above the operation of Adam and Eve, who couldn't resist temptation. We have a higher version of spiritual technology. Therefore, we have no excuse and reasons for not drawing God's attention to earth.

CAPACITY TO INTERFACE WITH THE REALMS

I earnestly prayed that the church of Jesus would come to the full understanding of her identity. Man was created in the image and likeness of God (Gen 1:26-27). God is a Spirit, and it is only the spirit that can operate in the realm of the spirit. But for a spirit to operate effectively in the physical world (earth), the physical body would be needed. Therefore man was created as a full spirit being. For man to operate on earth, he was given a body to function well on earth, which makes him mortal with immortal capacity. God made him from the dust of the ground. The ground is so prophetic because man would definitely, constantly and continuously have something to do with the earth.

Therefore, the body created for the man was not what makes him to be man, but the Spirit of God in him. Even angels envy man, who was created in a special way to relate or interface with two realms perfectly. For instance, the Bible reveals that God came down in the cool of the day to relate with Adam and Eve. Please, pause a minute. Ask yourself how did God do it, since he doesn't have flesh like man, how could He work round the Garden of Eden? Also, where is the geographical location of the Garden of Eden on earth today? Every city and location mentioned in the Bible are still in existence till today. No geographical location on earth can clearly define the region of the Garden of Eden till today. Many scientists have done all they could to have a clue or an idea of the location of the Garden but no one has traced it. I have come to the conclusion that it's beyond a region. It is a realm.

You may be surprised to know that the Garden of Eden is not a geographical or a physical location, it is a realm, where God and man related well. This is where there is no hindrance between humanity and the Divinity. Let your mindset be adjusted today. You are a spirit man, you were given a body in order to relate with your world and you have a soul that will give account of how well you have carried out your assignment here on earth. Then why are you promoting your flesh instead of your spirit, which is your real identity? The church is not the normal set of people on earth, but the abnormal ones, whose operations cannot be decoded by the people of the world. To refer to someone as a spiritual person is rather a downgrading of identity. The devil is short changing men on a daily basis, taking the original identity and leaving the fake, making man to concentrate on the minor instead of the major. Therefore, to me, saying a man is very spiritual means that the man is very carnal, living in the reality of flesh (senses), but once in a while he exhibits some spiritual characteristics. It points to the fact that the man is more of carnal than living by the Spirit's dictates. I am not spiritual, but just a spirit being. It is rather a derogatory remark to say that someone is spiritual. Being spiritual is to exhibit some spiritual nature or features. But spiritual being does everything in the spirit form.

Beloved, the church has a unique identity which you and I possess. We must work on the reality of our identity. This is what the devil does not want us to do. You must walk in the reality of your identity if you are going to be effective both in heaven and on earth, growing into maturity where you can interface with the two realms. This has nothing to do with a big or little position or title. God wants to share His burden with someone; this can only come into a place of deeper relationship. You cannot know God beyond the relationship you have with Him. We need men who can invite God to come and dine on earth again.

THE LIGHT OF THE EARTH

The Bible says, "You are the light of the world- like a city on a hilltop that cannot be hidden"(Matthew 5:14). If movement will exist as part of the characteristics of living beings, light will be necessary for clarity and direction.

THE ILLUMINATION

The New International Webster's comprehensive Dictionary (Encyclopedic edition) defines an illumination as:

(1) The act of illuminating; a state of being illuminated

(2) Lighting up, especially for festal purposes.

(3) Mental enlightenment; impacted light; spiritual enlightenment.

You may be surprised to see that the dictionary also views the word illumination from the spiritual angle.

Darkness typifies evil. Light is the only thing that has been designed by God to subdue darkness. The appearance of light evacuates darkness automatically. Light and darkness were not designed to compete. Darkness can kill. It is the next thing to death. It makes life meaningless. The Church is designed to bring joy, happiness, brightness and life to the earth. It is not designed to be a frustrated set of people waiting for the day they would escape the world's mess. If that is what we are doing as the church, we are becoming irrelevant on the earth. And if we are no longer relevant to the place where God has placed us, we would still continue to be irrelevant even when we eventually get to heaven. The position of the church is very important to the earth. The earth has been loaded with different philosophies from the kingdom of Babylon. We as the church have the mandate to get rid of these wrong systems and enforce God's kingdom values on earth. The Bible already says that the right order will proceed out of Zion. (Isaiah 2:3)

THE DIRECTION

Apart from giving illumination, light also directs. Just as a life without a vision is dangerous, so is vision without direction meaningless. A direction can come in the form of information and revelation. All that the world has is information, and there is a limit to which it can take them. The church, however, is endowed with the capacity to relate to heaven and earth, having received the keys of the kingdom of heaven (Matthew. 16:19). The function of the church is to proffer solutions to the problems of the world system through the power of revelation so that many will be drawn to God's kingdom and glory will be given to Him alone. The reason the world is continuing to remain in a mess today is that the church cannot proffer the solutions that can fix the world's problem. Romans 8:19-22 says, "For all creation is waiting eagerly for that future day when God will reveal who his children really are..."

Isaiah 2:1-3 also records: This is a vision that Isaiah son of Amos saw concerning Judah and Jerusalem: In the last days, the mountain of the Lord's house will be the highest of the entire most important place on the earth. It will be raised above the other hills and people from all over the world will stream there to worship. People from many nations will come and say, Come; let us go up to the mountain of the LORD, to the house of Jacob's God. There he will teach us his ways. For the Lord's teaching will go out from Zion; His word will go out from Jerusalem."

The scriptures above are prophecies written concerning today's church. This church being described here will be the only one that has the keys to solve the world's problems. This points to the fact that if we can manifest our true identity, the world will seek help from you and me on their own accord; we would not need to plead with them. This, however, will only happen by revelation. This was what the church in the wilderness, shepherded by Moses, experienced when a pillar of cloud was leading it in the day and a pillar of fire in the night. This typifies (divine instructions) Revelation.

The potency of the light of the church should give direction and illumination to the world. Jesus did not say where the light of the church. Why? Light in the midst of the light is worthless. God wants us to direct the affairs of the political, economic and social sectors of our world according to His will. It is only by doing so that we would be fulfilling our mandate as the church of Jesus on earth.

Chapter 8

The Dead-Living Church

"It is impossible for a sick and dying church to heal a sick and dying world."

"When the governor saw what had happened, he became a believer, for he was astonished at the teaching about the Lord."
Act 13:12

There are three key words that make up the phrase "the dead-living church". Two of them consist of a compound word, "dead-living." From chapter one to chapter seven, we tried to establish and define what the church of Jesus ought to be. Having had a clear understanding of what the church ought to be, we can easily x-ray or examine ourselves as individuals or as a member of a local assembly to see whether we measure up to the standard of Jesus' church or we are patterned after the dead one.

The first question to ask is, "Is the expression "the dead-living church" correct? Can there be anything that is dead and yet is living? "Dead" means "not alive." Whatever is dead has no life and belongs to the pastor is no longer practicable or fashionable. "Dead" also means "finished." For instance, when a person says there are two dead bottles of wine on the table, what he means is that there are two empty bottles of wine on the table. "Dead" also means "being insensitive." This presupposes that certain parts of a man's body could be dead even though the man is still living. A person whose senses are dead may not be able to see, hear, smell or feel pain. Going by the above definitions of the word "dead", we can establish that an entity could be living and yet dead. This explains that a church could even be 95 percent out of order or purpose and is still carrying out many activities. Therefore, to perfectly understand this concept, it is very important that we look at certain characteristics of living things in relation to the living church.

CHARACTERISTICS OF THE LIVING CHURCH

It has been discovered that millions of atoms and molecules are arranged in an orderly and complex manner to produce a living organism. These organisms are composed of one or many cells that often require a lot of energy to stay alive. This constant supply of energy is what is needed to maintain a living organism. Hence, obtaining and using energy are important activities of living organisms. However, being active does not necessarily mean being productive. To be productive requires more than just being active. Don't forget that it is individuals that make up a church. Therefore, having a productive and fruitful church goes beyond just carrying out activities. If these activities do not produce results and influence the earth positively to bring glory to God, they are dead works. Therefore, we shall be considering below the general characteristics and processes of living things based on scientific explanation and then use these characteristics to explain the concept of "dead-living church."

NUTRITION

"And Jesus answered him, saying, it is written, that man shall not live by bread alone, but by every word of God. (Luke 4:4 KJV)

Just as bread is necessary for the growth of the physical body, the word of God is also necessary for the growth of the church. Jesus is saying that the physical bread is not enough because man is a spirit being that only lives in a body. The real man cannot exist or live too long without spiritual food, which is the word of God.

"...and the very words I spoke to you are spirit and life." (John 6:63). Life in the spirit can only be vibrant by taking the food that is meant for the spirit. A man may be physically healthy and yet dead spiritually. The church can only survive by feeding on the words of God in due season. Every living organism needs food to stay alive. It takes good food (balance diet) for the body to grow and derive energy to operate. Likewise a spiritual man can only survive on revelation (the inspired word of God). When a living being no longer feeds regularly, it is a sign that death is imminent. This also implies that a church that does not continue to desire fresh word from God will soon die, regardless of how active the people are physically. The "word" we are referring to goes beyond reading the scriptures religiously or reading it back to back. If it lacks the inspiration of the Holy Spirit; it is just a mere literature. Moses, Joshua and the prophets did not have Bibles, but they worked with the freshness of God for every season and issue. Also, having the ability to feed is not enough; the diet must be balanced and fresh. If you feed on stale food continuously, you will suffer from malnutrition and subsequently die. The word God spoke to you yesterday may no longer be competent to handle today's crises. David learnt to always inquire of God before taking any action. This is the pattern heaven also expects from the church. The church is not supposed to be governed by experience or professional ideas, but rather by prophetic revelation.

RESPIRATION

All living organisms respire. Respiration is the release of energy from the breakdown of food substance within its body. The process usually needs oxygen, which the organism must get from its surroundings while it gives out carbon dioxide from the use of other living things like plants. It is not enough to be full of the word; we must also be filled with the Spirit at all times. Just as the physical body cannot do without breathing, physical air, the spirit man cannot also do without the Holy Spirit. It is through the help of the Holy Spirit that we are able to live the Christian life. The Holy Spirit is our strengthener. As we feed on the word of God, the Holy Spirit breaks it down for us in an easily digestible way that we can apply to our day- today life. There are many churches today that feed on the word, but do not allow the flow of the Spirit. Such churches can also be regarded as dead because it is only the Spirit that gives life. The letter kills.

EXCRETION

Excretion is the removal of unwanted substances from within the body of a living organism. These unwanted substances are known as waste, and they are usually toxic. What this means is that the church must constantly do away with things that defile. Jesus said, "Every plant that my Father in heaven has not planted will be rooted out." There are so many things within the church today that need to be purged out. They include sin, idolatry, heresies, traditions of men, and so on. The church must also get rid of stale bread. The fact that God revealed or spoke to you about an aspect of your organization's activities some years ago doesn't mean it can deliver any longer today. When Jesus declared woes on the Pharisees, the Sadducees and the teachers of the law in the book of Luke, He knew that their modus operandi was once endorsed by heaven, but the new move of God had made them obsolete. The old dispensation of the law (old technology in the spirit) is no longer relevant on earth to what God has in the spirit of the new age. Therefore, whatever you're still holding to, which heaven has regarded as outdated would no longer hold sway in the new agenda of God for planet earth.

A living church must be very flexible with the Holy Ghost. When a stereotype operation locks the Holy Spirit out of the church, the tradition (men's ideology or yesterday revelation) takes the place of the new revelation. Let us be careful the way we build what God has committed into our hands. God does not change, although His technology changes depending on the season. He made the first man (Adam), by creating a mature being. After the fall of man, he changed His technology to that of growing a man from the childhood stage to sonship or adulthood. We can relate this to a regular program that is producing what you consider as a result but which God has no hands in. Searching the mind of the Spirit today will make all the difference in your life. There may be something new in the Spirit he wants to make known to you.

MOVEMENT

All living organisms have the ability to move either part or all parts of their bodies. Generally, animals and human beings can move themselves from place to place. How does this apply to the church? The church will be able to fulfill her major cause on earth if she has the ability to migrate with God to places. The church is yet to come to an understanding that there is a destination; we are like pilgrims on a journey. There shouldn't be any side attraction or distraction that should affect a purposeful pilgrim from his journey. Our mind should be set permanently on our journey and the destination defined by God. The Bible says that we are moving from glory to glory and each level of the glory has certain level of things it can accomplish for our God on earth. God had determined the capacity and the weight of each level of the glory. If this is the case, why should our lives, businesses, marriages and ministries be permanently built where God was many years ago, without any idea of where He is presently? This was the paradigm of the Pharisees who were too used to a particular way God did things without any sensitivity of God's new moves on earth.

"Who will bring me into the strong city? Who will bring me into Edom?"(Psalms 60: 9 KJV)

God is a God of the journey, that's why man interprets his new operation in the Spirit as a movement. Every new move of God requires men and women that can align themselves to mind and the will on earth. A rigid and stagnant person or a church can't fulfill His mandate for any season and generation.

SENSITIVITY

A living organism is sensitive. It is able to detect and respond to changes within its surroundings and within itself. This ability is known as response to stimuli. Pains, changes in temperature and light intensity are examples of stimuli. How do these apply to the church? The last chapters tell us about the authority of the church over her environment, both spiritual and physical. The early church was very sensitive to its environment such that there was no platform for demonic operations within the church. The present church has failed to realize that even the devil's technologies of deception and perversion have long changed. We are still adopting the techniques of the seventeenth century to carry out evangelism and discipleship and to fix all other areas of our lives in the twenty first century. Heaven has changed the strategies long ago, but the Church is still at the same point that God was years ago.

The church is no more sensitive to the environment where she has been placed to control and dominate. It is so bad that the society is being polluted and the Church is not even aware of the fact that things have gone out of hand. This was the same problem that Adam and Eve had. They were so insensitive to their environment that they gave heed to the lies of the devil. The church of Jesus was designed to be very sensitive.

GROWTH

All living organisms grow. Growth primarily means increase in size, which is usually accompanied by the development. Development often refers to a change in form and abilities.

"Now these are the gifts Christ gave to the church, the apostles, the prophets, the evangelists and the pastors and teachers. Their responsibility is to equip God's people to do his work and build up the church, the body of Christ. This will continue until we all come to such unity in our faith and knowledge of God's sons that we will be mature in the Lord, measuring up to the full and complete standard of Christ" Ephesians 4:11-13

The Church is yet to perfectly understand that there is a difference between growth and development. For instance, the fact that an economy is growing does not mean that it is developing. It is possible for someone to experience growth without development, but there can never be development without growth. Development is therefore essential to growth. The Holy Spirit must be allowed to have His way in our lives, if we are going to achieve tremendous growth that will produce tangible fruits for the world to see.

Also, the fact that a person is fat does not mean that he is healthy. Growth is based only on the wings of the Spirit (the principles and patterns of God). It can come via popular ideas and what men claim to be in vogue. For many years, I have a problem reading books written by any author that is referred to as a "pastor of the largest growing church". The question I asked is this: how do we measure the fastest growing church (local assembly)? Who determines the parameters? Beloved, don't be deceived, growth goes beyond the large crowd that we are pursuing today. The true growth is measured by the weight and the size of Jesus that is formed in us and each member of our congregation/ fellowship.

It is vain to continue gathering multitudes that cannot hear God themselves, have dominion over sins, walk in the Spirit and love God and one another genuinely. We can see a perfect example of growth and development in the early church. They were people who lived a life of love. None lacked among them. They shared things in common; they took responsibility for one another's lives. They served the purpose of the kingdom, they reached out to their world and they understood that success and achievement go beyond heaping treasures to themselves. This is the kind of growth that the church of Jesus requires. It is not measured by the number of branches and crowd. These may not be bad, but it is important to make growth (Christ being fully formed in us) a priority. This will reflect in every of endeavor and operations of men. Our life styles will bring glory to God on earth if we are truly growing.

REPRODUCTION

All living organisms reproduce, that is, they give birth to offspring that look exactly like them. Through this process, they are able to preserve the existence of their generation. Genesis 1:28 says, "God blessed them and said, 'Be fruitful and multiply. Fill the earth and govern it. Reign over the fish in the sea, the birds in the sky, all the animals that scurry along the ground." In John 15:16, Jesus said, "You didn't choose me. I chose you. I appointed you to go and produce lasting fruit, so that the Father will give you whatever you ask for using my name."

God places so much importance to reproduction. He did not just create Adam and Eve to work on earth till the time He would take them to heaven (even though the coming of Jesus after the fall of man has changed the first story). One principle, we could bring out of the first man even after his fall is the responsibility assigned to him here on earth to reproduce after his kind. God wants to see the earth filled with His people like Himself. It is sad that the church finds it so difficult to differentiate from the world today. It has become so interwoven with the world that she is losing her influence in the world. No doubt, we are gathering crowds and multiplying church branches, but the kingdom values are decreasing daily. Does this perplex you? The church is living by the sense knowledge today and reproducing after the flesh.

The church of Jesus is a spiritual entity, which has the ability to relate to the world. It was established to influence the world with the kingdom values, not to be polluted or conquered by the world or the Babylonian system. There is a great concern in the heart of God for His church. Therefore, when any of these seven characteristics listed above are not in place in any church, it means nothing but death at work.

Chapter 9

Jesus Outside The Church

"There is no door that can be too important for me to hang on if unrighteousness is involved. I do not care what benefit may be attached to it."

"Honesty guides good people; dishonesty destroys treacherous people. Riches won't help on the Day of Judgment, but right living can save you from death".
Proverbs 11:3-4

One of the greatest pains that can ever be inflicted on a man is for him to labor to build a house and in the end he is shut outside. It would also be painful when a man designs a concept and it ends up working against his original intention. We should actually take into cognizance that Jesus was very enthusiastic when He said, "I will build my church." The question to be asked now is: "Where is Jesus within His church?" As we journey towards the end of this book, we would be able to see what led to His exit from His church.

We shall be looking through the book of Revelation chapter one to three. We shall see the position and the movement of Jesus within the church before He ended up outside.

THE SPIRIT WITHIN THE CHURCH

The church Jesus built is spiritual. This means that without a consistent relationship between the church and Jesus, there can't be a life in the church. It is a great error and lack of understanding that make ministers in the local assemblies to always say, "As we come into the presence of God" or "Let us invite the Holy Spirit into our gathering." This only suggests that such gatherings are dead. The Spirit should automatically be present whenever and wherever the church gathers. Let us take a look at some of the things God revealed to the Apostle John in the book of Revelation.

"It was in the Lord's Day, and I was worshiping in the spirit. Suddenly, I heard behind me a loud voice like a trumpet blast. It said "Write in a book everything you see, and send it to the seven churches in the cities of Ephesus, Smyrna, Pergamum, Thyatira, Sardis, Philadelphia, and Laodicea." (Rev 1:10-11).

The Revelation of John the apostle gives us the true picture of today's church. We are going to briefly look at where Jesus is at this dispensation and operations of the churches on earth today.

God is a Spirit and He can only relate to us through His identity. He is not really concerned about the activities that we engage in; He is more particular about the intents of our hearts. In the Revelation, God showed John both the things that are now happening and the one to happen thereafter (Revelations 1:19).

THE BEGINNING OF THE JOURNEY

The journey that led to the exit of Jesus from the church went through different stages until He could no longer cope with the environment and there was no place for Him. Do not forget that the church is an assembly that has a general collective decision making body and meeting point of worship called the temple in the Old Testament, but it has now been redefined in the new dispensation (New Testament) to be you and me. Let's summarize the stages He went through from the inner part of the church to the outside. The seven churches in Revelation 1:11-2 and 3 typify seven different churches in our world today. And we shall see where we belong in the seven churches.

TYPE 1: THE CHURCH OF EPHESUS

"I know all the things you do. I have seen your handwork and your patient endurance. I know you don't tolerate evil people. You have examined the claims of those who say they are apostles but are not. You have discovered they are liars. You have patiently suffered for me without quitting." Revelations. 2:2-3.

Oh! See what good commendation the church of Ephesus had from the Lord: they endured the challenges and tolerated no evil people; they welcomed only people that were ready to abide by God's standard into their congregations; they preached and lived only by God's pattern. They suffered for Christ. What else can a man do for his God than to stand for righteousness? Let's see the next two verses.

"But I have this complaint against you. You don't love me or each other as you did at first! Look how far you have fallen! Turn back to me and do the work you did at first. If you don't repent, I will come and remove your lamp stand from its place among the churches." (Revelations 2:4-5

WHAT TO NOTE ABOUT THE CHURCH OF EPHESUS

"You don't love me or each other as you did at first."

Love is an affection that comes from the heart and is expressed outwardly. God is not looking for people that would be afraid of Him or of His judgment. He is looking for those who will love Him. He needs our love. A man may keep away from fornication, lying and other sins, not because he loves God, but because he doesn't want to miss heaven or end up in hell fire. This should not be the right motive of following God. The earth is our place of primary assignment; we should not be in a hurry to go to heaven. We should obey God because we love Him. We should not allow idols to occupy where God ought to occupy in our hearts. What are the idols? They include money, fame, success and even failure. They could also be positioned, career, spouse, children, outward appearance, work, knowledge, fashion, cars or people. The truth is that you know your own idols. Jesus said when we begin to lose our love for Him, other people will take our place among the churches i.e. our lamp stands will be removed.

Therefore, what God requires from us is a life of steadfastness and genuineness. These are some of the things that can retain him in our lives, otherwise we would become empty as time goes by. Jesus concluded his message to the church of Ephesus by saying:

"Anyone which cares to hear must listen to the spirit and understand what he is saying to the churches. To everyone who is victorious, I will give fruit from the tree of life in the paradise of God."

TYPE 2: THE CHURCH OF SMYRNA

"Write this letter to the angel of the church in Smyrna. 'I know about your suffering and your poverty, but you are rich! I know the blasphemy of those opposing you. They say they are Jews, but they are not, because their synagogue belongs to Satan. Don't be afraid of what you are about to suffer. The devil will throw some of you into prison to test you. You will suffer for ten days. But if you remain faithful even when facing death, I will give you the crown of life." Revelation 2:8-10

Material things or acquisitions are not the true standard of measuring divine (kingdom) riches on earth. The devil may make the church feel very sad at a point when divine resources are yet to be translated or transferred into a physical reality. The fact that you, as a church, are experiencing shortage does not make you a poor person. Even those who are very rich, sometimes experiencing a period of lack, and such experience does not make them to fall into the category of poor men. People who are oppressing others with physical possessions, who claimed to be from God are not but belong to the devil. Suffering, challenges and attacks of the devil, an affliction that doesn't give us liberty to express our freedom (prison), which could differ from person to person, are not enough reason to deny God or yield to the devil's ideology. They have only come your way to test you before heaven could trust you to the next level. Abraham was tested with Isaac, his son, the most precious and valuable thing to any father. He didn't fail, and then he was entrusted with the capacity to be the father of many nations.

Everything we see as trials and challenges as a church are things that test our maturity and that also fashion us to the standard that God can really depend on. Until you are processed, you can't possess the kingdom. Many believers and other church folks have turned back to serve other gods today because of little challenges. These are men and women who are serving God as if He was a "father Christmas" (people that come to God for what they can only get from Him). He can do anything but he will not do everything. There is a time and season under the heaven. You can't pressurize him either; He doesn't need your attestation and approval to be God. Plus, you and minus you, He is God. He has only chosen to be God with us. Our mind must change about Him today.

But if you remain faithful even when facing death, I will give you the crown of life." The question is this: would you jump the processing of God? He alone determines the parameter.

Anyone with ears to hear must listen to the Spirit and understand what he is saying to the churches. Whoever is victorious will not be harmed by the second death.

Beloved, I suggest at this point in time that you pray that God himself will help you and keep you faithful in the midst of challenges like Daniel and the other three Hebrew children. What would be your testimony?

TYPES 3: THE CHURCH OF PERGAMUM

"Write this letter to the angel of the church in Pergamum. 'I know that you live in the city where Satan has his throne, yet you have remained loyal to me. You refused to deny me even when Antipas, my faithful witness, was martyred among you there in Satan's city. But I have a few complaints against you. You tolerate some among you whose teaching is like that of Balaam, who showed Balak how to trip up the people of Israel. He taught them to sin by eating food offered to idols and by committing sexual sin. In a similar way, you have some Nicolaitans among you who follow the same teaching. Repent of your sin, or I will come to you suddenly and fight against them with the sword of my mouth. Anyone with ears to hear must listen to the spirit and understand what he is saying to the churches.'"

John was hereby revealing a particular stage where the church would live in difficult times. He describes a time when all manner of lifestyles, cultural systems, fashions, philosophies and religions will spring up. There will also be social and economic pressures. By the grace of God, the Pergamum church was able to survive these things.

One of the problems of this class of church, however, is a leadership problem. John describes the Pergamum church as a group of people that had grown to be leaders and teachers in the house of God, men who had reasons and scriptural backup for every evil they were committing. Verse 13 shows us that they started earlier with good intentions, but along the line their actions became perverted. The spirit of Balaam suddenly took over their activities. This spirit makes men to use God's anointing against His will. It is a spirit of greed, a spirit that first thinks about what he can get into the ministry or service before rendering it. The spirit of Balaam is also a spirit that does the work of God while nurturing a personal agenda. It operated in the Pergamum kind of church. Also, in verse 15, Jesus rebuked them for harboring those who practiced the doctrines of the Nicolaitans. In verse 16, He admonishes them to repent otherwise He would come upon them suddenly. Today, many are dying because they practice evil doctrines.

TYPES 4: THE CHURCH OF THYATIRA

And to the angel of the church in Thyatira say: These things says the Son of God, whose eyes are like a flame of fire, and his feet like polished brass: I have knowledge of your works, and your love and faith and help and strength in trouble, and that your last works are more than the first. But I have this against you, that you let that woman Jezebel say she is a prophet and give false teaching, making my servants go after the desires of the flesh and take food offered to false gods. And I gave her time for a change of heart, but she has no mind to give up her unclean ways. See, I will put her into a bed, and those who make themselves unclean with her, into great trouble, if they go on with her works. And I will put her children to death; and all the churches will see that I am he who makes search into the secret thoughts and hearts of men: and I will give to every one of you the reward of your works. But to you I say, to the rest in Thyatira, even to those who have not this teaching, and have no knowledge of the secrets of Satan, as they say; I put on you no other weight. But what you have, keep safe till I come. He who overcomes, and keeps my works to the end, to him I will give rule over the nations, And he will be ruling them with a rod of iron; as the vessels of the potter they will be broken, even as I have power from my Father: And I will give him the morning star. He who has ears, let him give ear to what the Spirit says to the churches. Revelations 2:18-29

Jesus began by commending the church of Thyatira for their love towards God and humanity, their patience and endurance. However, in spite of their strengths, Jesus was not well pleased. The virtues He mentioned and commended them for in verse 19 are the things they themselves could have been proud of, thereby leading to self-righteousness. It is important to know that God has a standard of righteousness and He is the only one who has the yardstick for measuring that standard. The Thyatira Church was guilty of permitting the spirit of Jezebel to operate amongst them freely. Jezebel, being referred to here, is not just a woman or a set of women, but a spirit that causes pollution, intimidation and manipulation. It is not solely feminine, although it is more pronounced in women. The spirit also expresses itself through men.

Oftentimes, people attach the operations of Jezebel to a particular way of dressing. The fact, however, is that it seldom manifests in that form. It is a spirit; spirits have no gender. When you see people weeping because they do not want to be judged after committing an offense, so that they could receive undue sympathy and forgiveness, it is the spirit of manipulation in action and it is also one of the operations of Jezebel. There are many who come to the house of God today with a heart of deception and not for the purpose of fellowship. Today, some come into an assembly (to be part of the church) for the primary purpose of choosing a good spouse. Some come just to get connected to specific people, some need a new relationship while some need job or contracts. Some simply prefer the flavor of a particular assembly: the corporate image, music, dressing, building structure, sound effects and so on. They do not come for the purpose of ministering to each other and unto God. They do not gather together as God's ambassadors take decisions and responsibilities on issues that concern their communities, societies and the kingdom of God at large.

The spirit of Jezebel is one that also promotes immorality in the churches today. Beloved, do you critically observe the rate of sexual immorality in the churches today? Do you know that even some ministers are fully involved in this immoral act? Are you aware that some churches are stylishly accepting homosexual practices while ministers are getting involved in it? Do you know that divorce has become an acceptable doctrine in the church of Jesus Christ today? All these are works of the spirit of Jezebel. When a minister, either male or female is manipulating people's hearts towards himself or herself instead of towards Jesus Christ, the Head of the church, it is the operation of the spirit of Jezebel.

When the churches that are supposed to compliment each other are now intimidating and competing against one another, it is the spirit of Jezebel at work. The spirit of Jezebel is the spirit of falsehood and hypocrisy that has eaten up the lives of many in the church today. Jesus is warning and calling those who fall under this category to genuine repentance, otherwise He will strike them all with death.

TYPE 5: THE CHURCH OF SARDIS

"Write this letter to the angel of the church in Sardis. This is a message from the one who has the sevenfold spirit of God and the seven stars. I know all the things you do, and that you have a reputation for being alive but you are dead. Wake up! Strengthen what little remains, for even what is left is almost dead. I find that your actions do not meet the requirements of my God. Go back to what you heard and believed at first: hold to it firmly. Repent and turn to me again. If you don't wake up, I will come to you suddenly, as unexpected as a thief. Revelation 3: 1-3

The perfect way to describe the Sardis church is that it was a very religious church, full of activities that were without accurate alignment with the will of God. It practiced idolatries in disguise.

The Sardis type of church is one with a full operation of religious spirit. The religious spirit is a dead spirit. Jesus has not called us into a religion, but into a relationship with the Father. Religion is what man designed for himself to seek and get God, although it is futile because God is a spirit. A man that operates through his senses alone cannot get God. A true relationship is a two-way interaction between God and man, which gives room for feeling, talking, hearing and seeing. Religion entails having a form of godliness, observing laws and ceremonies that men believe can please God and deliver them from the wrath to come, but denying the power of godliness.

Revelation 3:1 also describes dead works, as activities that have no significance in the spirit. It says, though you have what it takes to be alive, by the works of your hands, you are dead. True worship can only come from a heart that is alive to God while a dead worship from a heart that is religious. This class of church, though exists, is already dead because the purpose for which she has been designed is not being fulfilled. God is still expecting the awakening of the remnant of this church, although the remnant left behind is almost dead too (Rev 3:2).

Verse 1 also makes it known that the mode of worship in this class of the church does not meet God's requirement. Jesus warns this type of church to stop, and turn back to what she initially heard and believed so that she could hold firmly to it. The only way this church can get out of her mess is to cease from all the dead works and the man- made methods of worship (religion), seeking only to worship God in spirit and in truth. Unless this happens, sudden destruction from the Lord will be inevitable. The Lord Himself testified that as bad as the state of this church was, there were still few within it that had not touched evil. The Lord promised that such would walk with Him in white robes because they were worthy, and that their names would also remain in the book of life. The only way out of destruction is that churches must understand the mind of God per time.

THE CHURCH OF PHILADELPHIA

Write this letter to the angel of the church in Philadelphia. "I know all the things you do, and I have open a door for you that no one can close. You have little strength, yet you obeyed my word and did not deny me. Look, I will force those who belong to Satan's synagogue these liars who say they are Jews, but are not to come and bow down at your feet. They will acknowledge that you are the one I love. "Because you have obeyed my command to persevere, I will protect you from the great time of testing that will come upon the whole world to test those who belong to this world. I am coming soon. Hold on to what you have, so that no one will take away your crown. All who are victorious will become pillars in the temple of my God, and they will never have to leave it. And I will write on them the name of my God, and they will be citizens in the city of my God the New Jerusalem that comes down from heaven from my God. And I will also write on them my new name. Anyone with ears to hear must listen to the Spirit and understand what he is saying to the churches. Revelation 3:7-13

The Philadelphia Church in our contemporary world represents the churches that have been perfected in love and in the knowledge of God. The word Philadelphia means "brotherly love." These are churches with high reputation, though they do not have much strength. They may not be popular, they may not have many members and supporters, they may not even have all the required resources to propagate the gospel, yet they are ready to do the will of God. Verse 8 says, "You have a little strength, yet you obeyed my word and did not deny me." The same verse serves as an encouragement to those who are passionately doing the will of God to continue. God is very much aware of your struggles and challenges in following the right paths and refusing to deny Him. We should learn a great lesson from here that God is more interested in building with accuracy than in building for the purpose of gathering multitudes. We can also see from the same verse that God is not only interested in efficiency but much more in effectiveness. This means that you can be zealously doing the right thing for God without doing things right. This also means that God does not just accept everything we bring before Him; we need to know His will before we can serve Him perfectly. Don't let mere zeal and motivation to push you into error. God is specific and He knows what He wants.

God is asking you today to do your best in serving Him according to the pattern He has revealed to you. Do not just seek men's opinions concerning His things. Do not seek for the approval and endorsement of men; just wait upon God. He is observing your sincerity and He will soon announce you to the world. As a matter of fact, you are His very hope for this generation. Keep on doing what is right in His sight. Never seek to please men. Hear what He says in verse 9: I will force those who belong to Satan's synagogue those liars who say they are Jews, but are not to come and bow at your feet. Those who are not serving God, but are building their own empires will be frustrated in this age and their frustration would compel them to come and submit at the feet of those who are building according to the pattern revealed to them.

It takes the working of God for those of Satan's synagogue (the temple of deception) to come and bow to a church with little strength. What this means is that God will soon make the unknown to become known. There are also some large congregations that have considered themselves as a strong church, claiming to be of God but are not; these ones will be exposed by the power of God in the days to come. Just watch out! Their long-term deceptions and their structures of falsehood will crumble. Many have already crumbled and many others will still be rendered ineffective, according to the word of God because He cannot continue to watch the ungodly to soil His holy name while His assignment is left undone. In verse 9b, Jesus says, "They will acknowledge that you are the one I love." This reveals that those who serve their own greed (god) but are claiming to be servants of God will come to acknowledge the hand of God upon those who have pledged their allegiance to the living God. Verse 10 forewarns us of the great time of trial that is coming upon the whole world to test those that belong to the world. The word here means the operating system of Babylon, which is totally in contrast with the kingdom of God. So a great calamity is coming that would touch every life, every sector and every organization. Any structure, ideal and existing systems of this world shall be tested by the Maker. This is the revelation the author of the book of Hebrews saw in 12:25-28:

Be careful that you do not refuse to listen to the one who is speaking. For if the people of Israel did not escape when they refused to listen to Moses, the earthly messenger will certainly not escape if we reject the one who speaks to us from heaven! When God spoke from Mount Sinai his voice shook the earth, but now he makes another promise: "Once again, I will shake not only the earth but the heavens also." This means that all of creation will be shaken and removed, so that only unshakable things will remain. Since we are receiving a kingdom that is unshakable, let us be thankful and please God by worshiping him with holy fear and awe. For our God is a devouring fire.

The only consolation for Philadelphia type of church is the promise of God after the shaking had taken place, which John called the testing of the whole world. This shaking will start from the church, beginning from the altar: the ministers, choirs, ushers and other workers down the line, every assembly shall be tested. The end will be the separation of the synagogue of Satan from that of Jesus. The true church will be exalted for the world to see. Also, don't forget that the last part of Hebrews 12 reveals that God is a consuming fire. This shows that all our work shall be tested by fire. Beloved, to which synagogue do you belong? What are you building with? Is it wood, clay, hay, iron, silver or gold? Fire shall test your work and mine. If it can still remain you will have a reward, if it does not, that is eternal loss.

THE OBEDIENCE OF PHILADELPHIA TYPE OF CHURCH

The greatest thing God showed me concerning the Philadelphia type of church was their obedience to God with their little strength. This is the type of church heaven is proud of. They were committed to heart service. Good commendation comes from the Lord who sees the heart of men. They were not like those who claimed they were Jews (the true assembly) whereas they were not. Jesus, however had to remind them that it was not enough to start well, but that it was also important to end well. He had earlier said, "Even the very elect might be deceived." But now He says, "I am coming soon. Hold on to what you have, so that no one will take away your crown." It is my prayer for you and my very self that our labor would not be in vain. It would be very painful when you labor in a wrong vineyard such that your reward is not different from that of the person who did not labor at all. Therefore, be careful how you labor because the one for whom you are laboring already has a defined specification that can never be lowered to any other standard.

Lastly, Revelation 3:12-3 says, "All who are victorious will become pillars in the temple of my God, and they will never have to leave it. And I will write on them the name of my God, and they will be citizen in the city of my God the New Jerusalem that comes down from my God. And I will also write on them my new name. Anyone with ears must listen to the spirit and understand what he is saying to the churches".

THE LESSON FOR PHILADELPHIA TYPE OF CHURCH

Verse 12 tells us that the victorious ones will become pillars in the temple of God. This means that there can never be victory without a battle. Then, what are the battles to be fought? They are the battles against the already existing systems and styles that the world had laid down as norms within the church- things that the church can no longer differentiate from the actual will of God. The rewards of becoming a pillar in the temple of God, that is, becoming a significant person, comes after heaven has tested and approved your work. Besides, having a good start does not guarantee a good end. Every stage of this journey is very important to God. Moses, for example, started well, but along the line, he missed the mark and the scriptures reveals that God killed him by Himself and Aaron took over from where he stopped.

Beloved, it doesn't matter how much praise you get for what you are doing for God, if your spirit does not follow God continuously to know His next step, you will miss it. Therefore, you must keep on praying and believing God for higher grace for each day and every other assignment. It is deadly too to get used to God's pattern and acts. It will only circumvent you from working by revelation rather than working with information that flies around. It does not matter how great you have built in the past, in as much as you can't birth or key into the present move of God, you are a failure as far as heaven is concerned. No matter how good you think you may be, God does not want you to think of Him. Don't let false teachers mislead you. What you need to do is to discover what He wants you to do. After this, all you need to do is to listen and follow. He who gave you the assignment has the blueprint, which you must adopt. Unfortunately, many of us today have left what God wants to build through us and are now building after the pattern of the mentors and authorities we have chosen for ourselves. I am not saying that having a mentor is bad. What I am saying is that once you begin to let men lead you, the uniqueness of God in you is lost naturally, and what He expects to achieve through your personality goes into oblivion. Don't forget that on the last day you and your mentor will stand to give an account of what you have all done. What will be your excuse?

The latter part of verse 12 says, "The victorious one will carry on their body the name of God and they will be citizens in the city of my God..." What this is telling us is that these ones would have the signature of God while on earth. Their lives would be endorsed by heaven just as Jesus' life and ministry were endorsed by God when He said, "This is my beloved Son hear him." The indisputable glory of God will bear witness to His calling upon our lives, when we press into this point without compromise. Becoming a citizen of the city of God gives you authority and privileges as a citizen. Now that you have passed all the test of being a citizen, the honor of the city (kingdom) becomes yours as well. You have all that you need; at this point you are a threat to the synagogue of Satan. He that has ear must listen to the Spirit and understand what He is saying to the churches.

THE TYPES 7: THE LAODICEA CHURCH

We need to be very careful as we look at the Laodicean church. This is exactly the state of the church today. The message to the Laodicean church is the message to the church in this dispensation.

"Write this letter to the angel of the church in Laodicea. I know all the things you do, that you are neither hot nor cold. I wish that you were one or the other! But since you are like lukewarm water, neither hot nor cold, I will spit you out of my mouth! You say, 'I am rich. I have everything I want. I don't need a thing! And you don't realize that you are wretched and miserable and poor and blind and naked. I advise you to buy gold from me, gold that has been purified by fire then you will be rich. Also buy white garments from me so you will not be ashamed by your nakedness and ointment for your eyes so you will be able to see. I correct and discipline everyone I love. So be diligent and turn from your indifference." Revelations 3:7-19

We have been able to establish that none of our works is hidden before the Lord. Our works go beyond what people see us do and condemn us for; it is our intentions and motives that matter. God is fully aware of all these things. The church of Laodicea represents a church that is uncertain, unpredictable, political and religious, operating by both the systems of Zion and Babylon. This type of church is a confused church. It seeks to serve both God and Mammon and it also desires a relationship with God while still being an ally in the world. Jesus said they were neither hot nor cold. In verse 16, He threatened to spit them out, and whatever God spits out of His mouth has become useless. It's no longer useful for the purpose it was originally designed. It becomes a waste.

In verse 17, we read of their seeming comfort because they trusted in riches. They got to a level where they began to be complacent, feeling that they already had all things and no longer needed anything. This type of church absolutely relies on the human resources, capital and financial resources at their disposal to get things done; they no longer put their trust in God. Seeking God's face today is no longer a thing of necessity. They no longer ask God for anything in prayer, neither do they exercise faith in Him anymore. They work by facts and reality and not faith. Mammon has possessed their souls. Verse 17b reveals that this class of the church never knew that they were miserable, empty, poor, blind and naked. They relied only on the arms of flesh and the power of their senses. In verse 18, Jesus advised them to humbly come unto Him to buy gold that had been purified by fire. This gold symbolizes the true values of the kingdom that have been tested to withstand the challenges of the time. He also counseled them to buy white garments from Him to cover their nakedness. The white garments mean the righteousness that comes only from Jesus, not by any works. He also recommends ointment for their eyes so that their eyes of understanding could be enlightened in order that they walk would by revelation and not to follow mere traditions or ideas the mind of fallen man.

There are many today who depend on head knowledge, acquiring doctorate degrees in theology rather than depending on the anointing of the Holy Spirit for revelation. Acquiring knowledge is very good, but we must be careful not to replace it with the leading of the Spirit. We cannot do the work of Jesus by mechanical formulae and human reasoning. It won't work; it has never worked.

Verse 19 shows that we should give thanks to God because He still loves us. It is he whom He loves that He corrects. It is however left for us to either accept His corrections or not. Every chastisement we receive that draws us nearer to Him is just a touch of His love and we should not despise such discipline. The later part of Verse 19 shows us that the true correction must occur consciously in returning to the original truth or else it will be distraction.

WHAT KEPT JESUS OUTSIDE THE CHURCH

Looking through the lifestyles and the predominant features of the seven types of churches we examined above, we would discover that the existing churches today are replicas of the churches of Ephesus, Smyrna, Pergamum, Thyatira, Sardis, Philadelphia and Laodicea. This is an eye-opener to us. We can now know the stages and the types of contemporary churches and where each of us belongs. We would see clearly that men are robbing Jesus, the Head of the church and that the church has been deviating gradually from the standard that He set from the beginning. The church of today professes the knowledge of God, but operates by the systems of Babylon. Jesus was completely sent out from His church by the people of the church and they are very comfortable having the Head of the church outside His church. Some do not know that this is a deadly situation because it cannot be so forever. If the Owner of the church is not willingly invited, He would come back forcefully to the church and many lives will go for it.

Look! I stand at the door and knock if you hear my voice and open the door, I will come in and we will share a meal together as friends." Revelation 3:20.

This is a very serious issue. What has sent Jesus out of his church? The first thing is that the environment is not conducive for Him. The language of the church has changed long ago. Everything about it has been modeled around man. It has graduated out of the school of the Holy Ghost and is now depending on constitutions and rules made by man. Men are elevating degrees above revelation. The flesh has taken over the place of the spirit (Galatians 5: 19-26).

Jesus is now out of the church and is at the door (outside the church) asking to be allowed into a place that is supposed to be His. We would summarize these things that sent Him out into seven parts. They are the spirits that need to be contended with in today's church.

The spirit of deception (Revelation 2:4-5)

The heart of the church of Jesus is going after another husband: money, people, fame, crowd, recognition, success etc.

The spirit of Balaam (Revelation 2:14)

This is the spirit that makes men to divert the grace and anointing of God for personal accomplishment; it is the spirit of greed, the spirit that makes a man to accept or receive the call of God with a hidden agenda.

The spirit of Nicolaitians (Revelation 2:15)

This is the spirit that manifests in the form of pride and subjection of the people of God. It is the spirit that demands service from the people of God rather than serving them. It is the spirit that is titled-crazy, forgetting that the power and the anointing of God do not lie in the collar, but in the calling.

The Jezebel spirit (Revelation 2:20)

This evil spirit has a stronghold in the church today. It works in both men and women. It is the spirit of pollution. The church today has been polluted with all kinds of doctrines and lifestyles for the purpose of seeking crowds, popularity and money. The spirit of Jezebel is a spirit of intimidation; it causes leaders to intimidate followers with their titles. It is a spirit responsible for sexual immorality that has become a license in the church today. The singles are committing fornication while the married are committing adultery and divorcing. Divorce, has become very common in the church. It is the spirit that promotes gift rather than fruits.

The spirit of deadness (Revelation 3:1)

This is the spirit that turns stones into bricks and revelations into the traditions of men. This is where rules and laws have taken the place of grace, intelligence the place of integrity and motivation the place of revelation. It is a Babylonian or worldly system- carnality at the highest order. It is a spirit of religion. 2 Timothy 3:5 puts it this way: They will act religiously, but they will reject the power that could make them godly. Stay away from people like that!

The chameleon spirit (Revelation 3:15-16)

This is the spirit of multiple identities. It is the spirit that promotes flesh in the morning and spirit in the evening. This is the spirit that operates in those who are looking for recognition and endorsement of men at all cost. It is a spirit of inconsistency and unpredictable lifestyles. This is what the church is filled up with today: lack of genuineness and integrity.

Spirit of Mammon (Revelation 13:17)

This is the spirit that has turned the church of God into a den of thieves. The church of Jesus has been taken over by the spirit of greed: many are lacking while some have a surplus. Mammon is the spirit that makes men to raise money even at the evangelical meetings, where unbelievers are supposed to be shown that salvation is free of charge. It is the same spirit that makes preachers to raise money false projects. The same spirit has blocked the hearts of the church from giving even when there is a genuine reason to give. It is the spirit that brings an unbalance message into the church, which turns Mammon to prosperity and prosperity to Mammon. This was the spirit that took over Gehazi in 2 kings 5:20-27. It is the spirit that falsely and forcefully collects gifts and raises money for projects that are not in line with the will of God.

These seven spirits have taken over the place of Jesus in our lives, ministries and the body of Christ in general. Until they are totally driven out of our assemblies, Jesus will not come to take His place. The question now is: "Are we ready to let go of whatever is taking the place of Jesus in our lives and allow Him to come in again? He is still waiting patiently to come in and take His people. He is standing at the door, knocking!

WHAT TO EXPECT WHEN JESUS COMES IN

There are things that must take place or happen when the owner of an apartment comes and takes over his house. For Jesus to come in, the door must first be open. Secondly, you can't open the door unless you can hear Him. If you sincerely invite Him, He would know and, instead of rejecting you He will come in and dine with you and share with you as a friend. But everything occupying

His place must be displaced before He will come. Those who overcome the deceptions of the already existing system will sit with Him on his throne just as He sat with His Father on the throne.

When Jesus regains His rightful place in the church, the whole world will know that something has happened. The truth is that regardless of how long you must have locked Him out, He is still interested in coming into his church. Beloved, take your pen and paper right now and write the things you must send packing out of your life, organization or ministry today. Do not procrastinate; otherwise the spirit of deception will circumvent you. Jesus wants His church back. Will you release it for Him or not?

I see in the spirit the bleeding heart of Jesus, wanting to restore his relationship with the church He died for. He came to his own people, and even they rejected him. But to all who believed him and accepted him, he gave the right to become children of God. (John 1:11-12).

It is highly painful for the Owner and Redeemer of our lives to now be at our doorstep asking to be let in. The most painful part is that the majority of people in the church only comes to Jesus for their own selfish interests. Nobody cares about His own concerns. The church has become a place where people buy and sell and get their needs met. People hardly come to show Him love like the woman that came to Him with the alabaster box of ointment (Mathew 26:6-13). Most people come to him just to receive. The woman with the ointment came to lavish something very costly just to minister to Jesus. This heartfelt love so got into Jesus' heart that He could not but comment on it. He said to those at the feast, "I tell you the truth, wherever the Good News is preached throughout the world, this woman's deed will be remembered and discussed."

It has now come to the point where whoever gives Him genuine love and acceptance will be given the right (license) to become a son of God. This means that as a child of God, every privilege from the Father will become yours.

Chapter 10

Hope For The Remnant

"I don't have a problem with people doing things that are displeasing to me as long as God is pleased. My Sadness arises when I'm pleased at God's expense."

"For we speak as messengers approved by God to be entrusted with the Good News. Our purpose is to please God, not people. He alone examines the motive of our hearts."
1 Thessalonians 2:4

As painful or hopeless as the church's situation may be, the fact remains that the counsel of God will always stand, regardless of whether the majority is doing His work its own way or not. It is common with God to always preserve a remnant in every generation. It is usually this remnant that He will equip and empower to carry out His purpose on the face of the earth.

"In that day the Lord will reach out his hand a second time to bring back the remnant of his people those who remain in Assyria and northern Egypt, in southern Egypt, Ethiopia, and Elam; in Babylonia, Hamath, and all the distant coastlands. He will raise a flag among the nations and assemble the exiles of the Israel he will gather the scattered people of the Judah from the ends of the earth." Isaiah 11:11-12

"Then the remnant left in Israel will take their place among the nations. They will be like dew sent by the LORD or like rain falling on the grass, which no one can hold back and no one can restrain. The remnant left in Israel will take their place among the nations. They will be like a lion among the animals of the forest, like a strong young lion among flocks of sheep and goats, pouching and tearing as they go with no rescuer in sight." Micah 5:7-8

The scriptures above confirm to us that the remnant will be fortified by God and they will do triumphantly as though they were a multitude. Their operation will be by the leading and guidance of the Holy Spirit. At Present, these sets of people are scattered all over the world. They may be unpopular- men and women of no reputation the society. Some of them may not even be recognized in their local assemblies and some may be members of assemblies whose operations have been disconnected from the Spirit of God. These remnants are the very few who are willing to hear God and do His will; they are men and women who are still being led by divine instruction and purpose.

We would see in this age that the remnant will be used by God to show forth His glory on the earth, regardless of their nationalities, cultural differences and complexion because they will all share the same burden the Holy Spirit in their hearts.

They will synergize for the King's purpose alone and God will begin to submit the destinies and the direction of the earth into their hands. One paramount thing you will discover in identifying this remnant is, that every of their operation will not involve any personal agenda but God's absolute will.

At Present, God is awakening and raising men whose hearts are right towards Him. He is confirming His word again, using the foolish things of the world to confound the wise. A lot of the unknown will be known and a lot of the known will become obsolete, just because they have become disconnected from the doing and following the moves of the Spirit of God.

GOD IS REBUILDING HIS CHURCH

The most exciting part of the whole story is that God will perfect the work He has already begun. It may look as though there is no more hope, as though the church has already derailed totally from the truth and the reality of God's purpose, but God can still accomplish so much with the remnant. God is raising men like Nehemiah, Daniel and Joseph in this age to lead this generation until the destination is reached.

"So the LORD sparked the enthusiasm of Zerubbabel son of Shealtiel, governor of Judah, and the enthusiasm of the whole remnant of God's people. They began re-building the house of their God, the LORD of Heaven's Armies." Haggai 1:14

In getting God's work done, the prophetic and apostolic offices will have to come alive again. It takes remnants that can partner with God to accomplish His tasks on earth. These remnants must be like Ezekiel, who, when he was taken into the valley of dry bones, still believed that God would raise them up to become a great army and God did. They must continue to pray and prophesy until the church of God emerges again with strong power and competence to get God's will established on earth.

Beloved, your ability to see what others cannot see will definitely inform your decision and reaction in the midst of global confusion, where men are living solely by their senses. The only men that can work with God as part of this remnant are men who can declare their stands against traditional and religious option for a revelation voice, by so doing the true church of Jesus will emerge and take her full responsibility and place on earth.

What you are doing in the name of God right now does not really matter; the question is: "Will you be part of the remnant God is counting on for the completion of His work on earth. Many people are working for God, but only a few are working with Him. It is only the few that are working with him that can please Him. Your idea may sound okay and look godly, but if the content has not originated from God you are only laboring in vain, building your own empire in the name of the Lord, and fire will definitely test your work. It is my heart prayer for you that your labor will not be in vain and that your motive will be right with God.

THE ROLE OF INDIVIDUALS

Beloved, what have you given to Jesus as a token of your love since you knew Him? This is a question you need to ask yourself. Is entering into His gates with thanksgiving becoming a challenge to you? Do you rather come with complaints, grumblings, demands, bitterness, unforgiveness and unbelief? Do you take time to remember the things God has done without requesting for them, or do you only remember what He has not done in your list of needs? What about your good health and that of your loved ones? Can you pay for the breath you are taking? Do you know that it is not everybody that can eat with ease even when there is an abundance of food? Do you know that it is not everybody that can feed themselves, even though they have varieties of food except they use certain medications or aids? Learn to give God your love and appreciation than only to demand for things.

Today, many have only come to church just to add to the number. They are yet to become citizens of the kingdom of God. They have not yet been converted. Many pastors now draw many people to themselves all in the name of church growth. They gather both sheep and goats in the same fold. Many do not know God, but are only familiar with their pastors and the rules of their local assemblies. It is sad that men of God are now taking the place of Jesus in people's lives. They enjoy having crowds of 'adult babies' who do not know their left from their right- members who will always have reasons to come for counseling, deliverance and consultations on all issues. By keeping people in ignorance, these men of God believe that they would not lose their relevance. They think that an ignorant set of people will always have reasons to depend on them. This class of the church can't even hear God because they are not taught to do so. It is even more difficult for them to know His ways. They only know the voice of their pastors so much that even if Jesus Himself were to speak to them, demanding their attention, they would first seek the approval of their shepherd.

Men of God and those who lead the people of God must bear in mind that they are only stewards over the flock of God. The fact that God has continued to keep quiet over certain issues does not mean that He is not watching jealously over the church. If you decide to sit as lord over God's heritage, you will put your life at risk. When He comes for His people, you will become a forgotten issue. The relationship you are holding on to at the expense of

Jesus can cost you your life and everything you have built around you. The Spirit is saying to you today, repent and sincerely turn a new leaf. Invite Jesus back to his rightful place in His church. Pray sincerely to Him as you confess your sins and ask Him to help you restore His people to Him. This is the injunction of the Spirit to them that have ears to hear.

YOU ARE THE CHURCH

Do not forget that from the very first chapter of this book up to this point, we have been trying to address and redefine what the church is supposed to be. We have also been able to see that the church Jesus Christ built and is still building is not a physical structure, but comprises me, you and a host of other people from all over the world. As an individual who has been set as a leader in the house of God, you have to make the necessary adjustments today in order to bring everybody, including yourself, to the lordship of Christ, who is the Head of the church. God can only use you if you submit totally to Him and prepare your mind to do His will only. Our lives are supposed to bring honor and not dishonor to God. If your life is so unpredictable, the Father will not be able to vouch for you. Remember that you were created to bring pleasure to God, and this can be achieved only when you live according to His will.

THE HEAVEN AND EARTH ARE WAITING

The church is the only hope of heaven and the earth. Every agenda of God will remain hanging in the spirit until the true church emerges and aligns herself to the exact will of God to bring about change on earth. It takes only the men who can download the mind of heaven to bring about change on earth. This means there must be an adjustment in our hearts also. Our spirit man must continue to pant after God so that heaven can entrust us with the resources and grace to establish the right order that the earth is waiting for. The whole world is in great confusion right now and it is the church of Jesus that holds the keys, and has the capacity by design to unlock the doors and release the solutions. This invariably means that until the church manifests the full capacity of her identity, the destiny of the world and the plans of God will continue to be at stake. Until the church steps into the level of maturity, the preparation for the return of the King would be delayed. The more we delay Christ's coming, the more we endanger the earth and the church as well. This is because things will continue to be tougher and more challenging by the day and the adversary of the people of God does not relent in his efforts. He knows that his days are short. The coming of the King is therefore tied to our ability and readiness to partner with God in seeing that every prophecy in His word is fulfilled.

"For he must remain in heaven until the time for the final restoration of all things, as God promised long ago through his holy prophets." Acts 3:21

This scripture reveals the mind of God to us that Jesus will not come until the fulfillment of every prophecy contained in the scriptures. Everything that fell from God's standard as a result of the fall of Adam and Eve must be restored to the original state after the restoration and resurrection of Jesus Christ. The Spirit of God made me to realize that the fall of Adam and Eve led to the fall of every other creature and the true resurrection reality of the church must restore the world to its original identity. This means that when the true resurrection power of Jesus is at work in the life of a man, his environment and everything surrounding him must obey his command. The lion was not designed to eat humans, neither was the snake created to bite them. It was the fall of man out of God's divine order that led to disorderliness in creatures, making them to begin to feed on one another.

Until Christ is fully formed in us as a church and until we attain the level of maturity that God expects us to attain, we would not be able to exercise full dominion on the earth. One of the reasons the second Adam, Jesus Christ, came was to restore dominion to man. The coming of Jesus was not just to redeem us so that we could escape to heaven. Much as heaven is important to us, we must not fail to carry out the responsibilities that God has assigned to us on earth. If we become indulgent and look forward only to the day when we would escape from this so-called "sinful world" to heaven, where there would be no more pain or sorrow, then we have failed. Heaven was not created for Adam and Eve; they were created to carry out responsibilities here on earth. A man that fails to fulfill God's purpose here on the earth may end up losing even heaven at the end.

Some years back, I questioned God about heaven and the attitudes of believers towards the place. He told me something I would never forget. He said, "Heaven is not a place of compensation for people who are losers on earth, but a place of rewarding those who fulfilled their mandate while on earth." This shows that compensation is only given as a consolation for something that is lost. For example, if you lost your insured car, after confirmation, your insurance company will compensate you. This is very much different from a reward, which you can get by being an outstanding member of staff or a committed stakeholder. This is what God told me: "When you are battered here on earth and you could not attain a position from where you can enforce the kingdom of God on earth, but you are only looking forward to the day when you will escape to heaven, you would have no reward with respect to the works you've done in the body while you are here on earth" (Revelation 22:12). Some will be so rewarded like the apostle Paul, Peter, etc. And some will be there also like Lazarus, who, though he made heaven, did not have anything to show for the works he had done for God here on earth.

Beloved, I do not know about you, but I desire rewards, not compensations. I want to be welcomed by Apostle Paul and others. I want them to congratulate me for being able to shine as a light in this crooked and perverse generation and also saving many others out of it. I don't want to hear, "Welcome, at least you made it." I want to hear, "Welcome, good and faithful servant. Enter into the joy of your Master." Take note of this: men may give you an award; it is only God that gives rewards. Men can base their awards on the things that are seen, but God looks into men's hearts. Peradventure you are working in an establishment where you are putting all your best and no one seems to be appreciating your efforts. Please, encourage yourself to do more. Man may owe you, but God will not. When God is set to reward you, you will see His hands working on your behalf either within the organization or somewhere else. Do everything as unto the Lord. You are accountable not only to man, but also to God. You are the ambassador that has been sent to that establishment. Many people must come to God because of your attitude and lifestyle.

Matthew 28:19-20 says, "Go ye therefore, and teach all nations, baptizing them in the name of the father, and of the Son, and of the Holy Ghost: Teaching them to observe all things whatsoever I have commanded you; and lo, I am with you always, even unto the end of the world." The reality of this scripture is far beyond our evangelistic approach. It speaks about living a positive and contagious life, such that anyone that comes across your paths must be affected by our kingdom values. The word baptizing in verse 19, in the original Greek translation is baptism, which means, "to make overwhelmed or fully wet." So when Jesus commanded that we should go and teach all nations and baptize them, what He means is that as we go out to the nations of the earth, starting from our family, neighborhood and our places of work, the lifestyle of the kingdom must be consciously impacted on the people around us such that they would be fully immersed in the same lifestyle and values.

In conclusion, beloved, I do not know how you see the church of Jesus Christ at this point. What do you consider to be your own responsibilities in advancing God's kingdom? Will heaven be able to count on you for the accomplishment of divine task and agenda in these days? Re-engineering is going on in the heavens; those that are not ready are being laid off and those with the right hearts are being recruited for the assignment. Don't forget that God can use anybody but He will not use everybody. The fact that He uses you or started with you doesn't mean He will continue with you. If your heart is no longer right and thirsty after Him and His will, He will find other vessels. I pray that the true burden of God's kingdom and His would fall upon your heart such that you would be restless until you align yourself to it. Make up your mind and take a decision today. Heaven is waiting for your choice. May the Spirit of the true revelation of God abide with you forever. Amen.

Watch out for the volume II of this book. The volume one you are rounding up now is a summary of what God revealed. Volume two reveals the true identity of the church of Jesus Christ, the coverage of the devil, the individual, corporate (local assembly), the state of the global church (the entire body of Christ) and the pictures in the agenda of God. It is entitled The True Church. God bless you!

About the Book

"The Dead-Living Church" re-defines the concept of the church (the true Ekklesia), her global positioning and her responsibilities according to the original intent of God. Jesus' declaration in Matthew 16, "I will build my church and the gates of Hell shall not prevail against it" far outweighs the theological assumptions and religious beliefs about what church is supposed to be. This book is not a product of professionalism; it is a prophetic release by the Spirit of the living God. The Church is not a denominational gathering of religious people, but the Ekklesia, the people called for an assignment, the assembly of legislating on behalf of God on earth. This book will take you through a journey. Its intent assuredly will awaken your spirit man to experience a paradigm shift from 'Churchianity' to that which is God's original intention.

About the Author

Isaac K. Arikawe is the Chief Responsibility Officer (CRO) of Revelation of His Kingdom Ministries (a non-denominational teaching ministry) and the International Coordinator for Kingdom School of Ministry (a non-denominational spiritual development platform for equipping God's people for ministry work globally).

Arikawe has an apostolic ministry: he is committed to the advancement of God's kingdom on the earth and the edifying of the body of Christ to perfection. He runs the Kingdom Schools of Ministry free of charge. He also speaks regularly at conferences, leadership meetings, and churches. His books have inspired many people globally.

He is married to Temitope, an admirable medical doctor with a deep passion for God's kingdom. Arikawe currently resides with His family in Lagos, Nigeria.

Other books by the Author

THE TRUE CHURCH

This book reveals what God expects from the church. It explains what Jesus meant by "I will build my church." The aim is not to write a critique, but to provide a standard of measurement as regards the state of the true church. The True Church is not Catholic, Protestant, Pentecostal, Charismatic, Gospel, Baptist, Methodist, African or any other name which is familiar to us. It is one which has put a priority on building, according to the pattern of heaven. ` This book will be a great eye opener for you. You will no longer strive in the flesh after going through it. The issue of competition, comparison, sense of inferiority and superiority complex, which are some of the distraction and strategies of the enemy, is exposed. You can't read this book and still retain your old mentality and operating system. Deeper truths and insights are made available inside the book.

THE EMERGENCE OF THE SONS

A child can only be born while a son would be made. A whole lot of processes are involved - transformation, changes, growth, capacity and character development before a child can come to the point of complete resemblance of his father. The responsibility and authority lies in the hands of the sons, men and women who have grown up to a higher intimacy and integrity of heart (people of high competence in the spirit). Their major burden and focus is to see the mind of the father being established on earth. They are men and women who are taking over nations and kingdoms of our Lord (those whose hearts have been knit to the Father's). The entire hope of the father lies in the hands of the sons. They are people that the Father can share His heart with. Sonship is not about age or title, but maturity in the spirit. Be ready to go through this process so as to be relevant in the plans and purposes of God.

BURDEN: A CATALYST FOR REFORMATION AND REVOLUTION

Every change, revolution and true reformation is a function of burden. Burden is anything that bothers you. The solution comes in the midst of great burden and concern. Nehemiah, Esther, Moses, Daniel and the Patriarchs of were able to do exploits just because they had great heaviness and burden in their hearts for discomforting situation. How many of us are ready to partner with God, making what hurts His heart to hurt our hearts? How many are ready to pray: "God, let everything that bothers you also bother me and let the burden of your heart be transferred into mine?" Until you get to this level, you would be living for yourself. The earth should not be expecting so much revolution and reformation until you and I begin to live beyond ourselves. We shouldn't be expecting a serious change except we pay the price. This book will surely open you up to a great burden in the spirit.

PROPHETIC LIVING

It is a book that talks about the needs of growing to a level of understanding the will and the mind of God per time. Deaf and dumb are not too far from deadness. Inability to hear and see from God's perspective is a function of spiritual deafness or an indication of being a bastard. It is not possible to walk in the accurate plans of God for our lives if we cannot hear from Him. God speaks per time, but until we tune our lives to this frequency, we would continue to hear wrong messages from wrong stations.

This leads to the process of doing the wrong things, embracing wrong values, regardless of how nice it might look like. This book exposes you to hearing God and the benefits of hearing Him per time. Your life will never remain the same if you read it.

PROPHETIC TRANSFER OF WEALTH

There are a whole lot of resources on wealth creation, strategies, the process of making, managing and retaining it, and so on. Among all these, the world's leading business schools and colleges, professors and expatriates have written and published so much through research and forecast, yet the reality of economic crises still has a global effect on the nations without any specific solution. Many have become jobless, while many great institutions have folded up. This is not the devil at work per se, but another way of God's involvement in the affairs of men. Only those that know their God on the last day shall be strong and do exploits. There is going to be a separation between goats and sheep, between sons and slaves. Heaven is raising the end time financiers for the sake of the kingdom. There is an outpouring of grace and anointing for unusual wealth creation, transfer and management on the connected saints of the last days. This book reveals the agenda of heaven on this issue and how to be qualified to be a partaker.

THE ACCURATE IDENTITY

Many lives have been short-circuited. It is the greatest desire of the enemy to ensure that the saints live outside their true identities. Our position in the spiritual realm is a function of the identity we carry. The impact of a man on earth is a function of his identity in the spirit. Also, the power and forces on earth and in the heavenliness are determined by the authority we have in the spirit. It is not a function of positions. Accurate identity talks about walking in the reality of redemption. Our position in Christ and our weight in the spirit are part of the things that determine our true identity. This book will provoke you to build a life in the spirit so that you can be relevant in God's move.

BUILDING FOR GLOBAL IMPACT

Man, as an offspring of God, was originally endowed with the capacity and ability to operate without any limitation of any geographical location. It is an aberration to creation and the purpose for man as a spirit being to be limited by some factors. Man was originally designed with external software that has the ability to fix national and global issues. This means that the value of every true man should be measured by his global impact. In every man lies a hidden sound that needs to be globally echoed or heard. This book will open your eyes and propel you to building for global impact.

KINGDOMIZING THE EARTH

The earth is the only place that the awesomeness of God can be expressed. The true citizens of the kingdom live consciously everyday with this mentality. If the glory will go to God from the earth, it must be by the activities and operations of the saint through their individual callings and specialization. Up till now the earth has been forcefully hijacked, wrongly colonized, subjected and controlled by Babylonians (wrong hands). This will continue until the sons of the Kingdom arise. This book reveals much expectations and responsibilities and consequently concerns the awakening of the kingdom citizens to their God-ordained calling. The true kingdom values must swallow up the Babylonians systems. Every opposing kingdom must be subdued and colonized for our King. This book is an eye opener and a call to contention.

OTHER BOOKS

8. The Church and the Rock (The Remnant Church

9. Prophetic Leadership

10. Apostolic Fatherhood and Mentoring

11. The Portrait of a Man of God

12. The Apostolic Rescuing of Soul

13. The Prophetic Compass of the Last Days Church

14. Understanding the Moves of God

15. Adam and Eve: Parable for Divine Union

16. The Messenger and the Message

17. Christ: The Pattern Son

18. Nehemiah: Pattern for True Apostolic and Prophetic Ministry

Kingdom School of Ministry

Introduction

The Kingdom School of Ministry is an offspring of Revelation of His Kingdom Ministry. Being a Ministry commissioned solely to the maturing (equipping) of the Body of Christ through our resources and materials—books and articles, Conferences, Seminars/Trainings, Media and Mobile Kingdom School of Ministries round the world.

The birth of the School: (KSM)

We are in a crucial season in the history of creation that times and events are testifying about. It is obvious that God is gradually bringing the age to a close. However, His intentions and purposes for creation must be fulfilled, though it tarries.

Many prophecies in regard to this have been fulfilled and some are still hanging in the air waiting for the fullness of time when the church (the Body of Christ) would rise up to her responsibilities in fulfilling the prophecies. This would be very impossible except she (body of Christ) has a prophetic understanding of the Seventh day (the completion and perfection of all things) agenda of God.

The question to be asked is, "Where is the church (the people) that will activate this prophetic agenda? Do we think this present church system, a mere religion, humanism, materialism and entertainment kind of Christianity can fit into this divine mandate?"

The Kingdom of God needs to be established, this was the center of Jesus messages on earth (scriptures), which must consequently reflect in every human endeavor.

Jesus gave the church a mandate, *"Therefore, go and make disciples of all the nations, baptizing them in the name of the Father and Son and the Holy Spirit. Teaching these new disciples (students) to obey all the commandments I have given you. And be sure of these: I am with you always, even to the end of the age."* (Matt. 28:19-20).

It is important to note that this command or mandate far outweighs our evangelical/charismatic assumption about the scriptures. It describes the entire process of turning a man into another being, **the express image of Christ** through proper training and discipleship.

The church would need more than the current knowledge to get this done. She needs the proceeding (current) truth from God to get this established. So therefore, the revelational knowledge is required.

God Himself testified to this truth, through the prophet Hosea in his book. *"My people are being destroyed because they don't know me….* Hosea 4:6 (NLT).

Meanwhile, this requires a progressive accession, continuous internal transformation, that will lead to outward transfiguration, where the scripture, Matt. 5:16 would be fulfilled. There is a need for the people of God to become apostolic/prophetic saints, regardless of our individual offices in the ministry gifts. The true Kingdom must be expressed in us through a **godly lifestyle, dying to self, power and authority, right knowledge, wisdom, understanding and revelation.** So the church of Jesus Christ (locally and globally) must take pleasure in growing up into maturity, the fullness of Christ which is the Christ-like expression that is needed for his hour.

It is imperative for everyone in the fold to discover and be empowered to fulfill their heaven-given purpose for the singular aim of advancing the Kingdom of Our King on earth. This burden gave birth to KINGDOM SCHOOL OF MINISTRY (KSM).

KSM is a kingdom-based Apostolic/prophetic educational initiative that is commissioned to midwife a last-day generation of saints by teaching and training believers and to serve as a grooming center for those that are called into a specific ministerial assignment of the last days. KSM will help them to clearly discover their purpose and empower them to fulfill it. It is a place where true kingdom-class leadership are formed or developed.

KSM does not have a particular denominational affiliate, rather she is ready to partner with any ministry, a local church, groups or individuals in any form of training, seminar, or schooling for their members, workforce or family for the purpose of kingdom expression.

KSM, also is not another type of theological school or one of the traditional Bible schools, rather this school is for spiritual development and to continuously plug men and women into the very current move of God and the emphasis for now.

This school by the aid of the Holy Spirit promises life transforming modules or curriculum, that you don't find in any traditional bible school. Rather, every grandaunt will wear a new spiritual nature and mentality.

OUR MISSION

To midwife the last day remnants that have been called and chosen to finish according to God's pattern and time table.

OUR PURPOSE

To educate, train and impact believers with relevant graces to build effective lives and ministries, by leading them back to the original intention of God for creation.

OUR OBJECTIVES

- To see the saints coming into maturity and the perfecting of the Body of Christ.
- To place great emphasis on the current move of God and His kingdom reality on earth.
- To introduce and fortify the ministry gifts with apostolic and prophetic graces.
- To raise a community of believers that can resist the influx of Babylon (the system of this world) within the Body of Christ and society.

OUR FOCUS (As school, training and seminar organizers)

- The kingdom concept
- The dynamics of God's moves and His seasons on earth.
- Kingdom-class leadership development.
- Original concept of the Ekklesia (church) on earth.
- Kingdom advancement and re-definition of the church growth.
- Maturity and finishing generation.
- The minister and the ministry.

OUR FACILITATORS

KSM is not a one man show. We are blessed with men and women of God within the five-fold ministry and marketplace apostles with a special understanding and grace in the Apostolic and prophetic dimension of Christ. Teachers with practical proof of godly lifestyles and testimonies whose burden goes beyond their denominational affiliates and personal gains.

We also raise teachers from our schools and train participants

Note: KSM is a FREE of charge school and our details are on our web page. www.ksm777.org.

Contacts:
5, Bariyu Street,
Off Holy Saviour Road,
Off Osolo way,
Isolo.

+234 803 575 0747, +234 809 1705 255
+234 807 1731 856
Contact @ ksm777@gmail.com; ksm777.org
www.ksm777.org

www.ingramcontent.com/pod-product-compliance
Lightning Source LLC
Chambersburg PA
CBHW052051070526
44584CB00017B/2133